ORDERED

STEPS

Ordered Steps

Nancy Wade Zappulla

Dedication

This book is dedicated to Dr. Barbara Nelle Ewell who has been my English professor for fifty years...and no, I didn't flunk. I just couldn't figure how to live without being in her class so I still am, and always will be, her student.

Forward

Dear Mrs. Zappulla,
    Thank you for being my teacher. Every time I came
in to your classroom, I always felt excepted (sic).
        Sarah Pollak,
           end of the year student review

There is nothing more intimidating than writing a forward for your former English teacher. This is coming from a person who's interviewed and written about everything from warlords in Sudan, presidents, and rock stars. Suddenly, even though I've been a writer all my adult life, I am worried about every single capitalization, punctuation, and possible grammatical error known to mankind. "How will she grade my work," I worry as I sit at the laptop sweating bullets, just like when I was in her eighth grade English class.

After years as a journalist, I reconnected with Mrs. Zappulla on Facebook. Oh, my! The memories from the year we had together in class came flooding back. Mrs. Z, as we were allowed to call her, was super cool. Somehow, she was all at once a ball of fire and a skillful comedian; a down-to-earth lady that you wouldn't want to meet alone in a dark alley and yet still the person you would most want to be by your side in a knife fight. I don't remember ever feeling that way about any other teacher.

This is the woman you will see in this book; pure unvarnished Mrs. Z. It's like taking a peek behind the curtain and glancing at the great and powerful Oz. These essays, filled with wit and soulful rumination, reflect her deep passion for teaching and her even deeper devotion to her faith.

Sarah Pollak-Hoffman is an accomplished reporter having worked for metro networks, BGEA, NPR, and CBN NEWS over the years. Sarah is currently working hard on her four most important little productions, also known as Mrs. Z's grandstudents.

Table of Contents

Clogs and Cars in the Spring

When people say, "What is the worst thing about losing your vision?" I know that they're expecting me to talk about having to change my career or being unable to see a sunset or some other monumental event. However, the worst part of losing my vision hasn't been those things at all, and my answers to that question have bewildered even me.

Because my visual condition is progressive, I have had time to get used to things falling out of my world in pieces, rather than in one big lump. I've had glasses, contacts, and other sorts of add-ons, and doubtless there are other gadgets waiting in the wings for me. It has added an element of intrigue to my life, trying to imagine what new thingamabob I will need tomorrow.

One element of life that couldn't be adapted or added on was my ongoing status as a driver. First, I couldn't drive at night, and then I began to notice pedestrians leaping onto the sidewalk as I drove past. It came to me then that it was time to park the car, but before I could suffer an emotional breakdown over that loss, the grand poo-bahs of vision explained that I could get amazing glasses (both in acuity and price) which could possibly enable me to drive. Time passed. I got the glasses, and no, it wouldn't work for me. DRIVING had become such a huge goal that I fully expected to fall apart when I couldn't manage it, even with the million-dollar glasses. Imagine my surprise when I felt just the tiniest stirring of regret and then life went on. I gave myself time to generate some serious wailing, but it just didn't happen. "Well," I thought, "I'm just one incredibly superior human being."

Within the same spring came another realization, which I think I had recognized but had been holding at bay with great devotion. One of the vestiges of my hippie days was my clogs. I had worn them in the ' 70's when they were cool, right through the ' 80's when they were weird and into the '90's when I amazed my students with my chic. Then, my vision made me unsure on terra no longer firma, and the clogs had to be abandoned for flat shoes.

Though I owned flats, my hands always lingered on the clogs, and each morning I waged a losing argument about wearing them. For some reason a lot of who I was had always been tied up with those wooden-soled shoes, and I couldn't even pass them along to Shannon, another clog aficionado. I missed the comfort of my clogs and the way they looked when I looked down at my feet, but most of all I missed being the teacher who wore clogs. There went another tiny piece of me.

Spring has always meant playing catch in the afternoon. My dad played on the farm team of a major league baseball team, and my Saturdays featured baseball games on TV with Dad providing the play-by-play. As soon as I was old enough, I began to play on a softball team, and even though I was never particularly talented, it was what I did in the spring. In my early years of teaching I coached, undoubtedly poorly but very sincerely, and even into my 40's I enjoyed watching the team practice, hoping to finagle a turn at bat. When my daughter signed up for softball, throwing and hitting and teaching her what I knew was a time of sweetness between us. Come the spring, and Claire and I would be in the backyard playing catch. Even with my deteriorating vision I could still manage with the orange softball, and so things were still okay.

But this spring has seen the end of my softball playing. Even with the bright orange ball, I can't judge the distances or move quickly enough to avoid line drives, and so there's been no catch for us. Claire looks for other partners without complaint, but unexpected tears appear whenever I have to explain my permanent spectator status. It is the most painful of my losses thus far, and though I know how silly it must seem -- a middle-aged woman crying over an old baseball glove and a scarred pink bat -- it still stabs.

Smarter folks than I must have the answer to this enigma, and perhaps one day I'll ask them. Right now, it seems right to grieve when Claire searches for a friend to play catch, and then when she finds one, I can't follow the game. Sages tell us that we must either run from a problem or fight it, but I think there's another choice. Maybe soon I'll find it.

Nancy Wade Zappulla

Be Careful What You Ask For

Jared,

When we were young, boys didn't ever jump rope much, I don't think, but we girls, we loved it. When you had one person on each end, then you could have one person jumping at a time or even two. I remember that feeling of standing, trying to get the rhythm of the rope so you'd know when to jump in. Oftentimes you'd hold your hands up, moving in time with the slap, slap of the rope on the concrete, trying to get the nerve to leap in without messing up in front of your friends.

That is the way I've been feeling since reading your request about me telling you what I think is important and what I teach. It hasn't been scary but rather trying to find the place to jump in. This is no small topic---what I think is important--- and as I've gone through my days, I have prayed and thought about where to begin and what to say.

Actually, it has been good for me to have to crystallize these concepts into organized, coherent wads; not so much fun, but good for me. Okay, I lied. I have felt honored by your request and not a little inadequate. So, I shall launch forth,

Ordered Steps

bulleting the ideas for the sake of organization.

None of what you'll read is exhaustive or even expert, but it is sincere and as far as I know, consistent with who God is and what the Word says.

- I believe in something I call "the integrity of the believer," which is the gap between what I think God is saying and what my Christian comrade is doing. For example, this comes into play when this person decides something is acceptable and I just don't see it. We're not talking murder or mainlining pharmaceuticals, but things less specifically addressed in Scripture. I have to give that other Christian permission to make a decision that is between them and God without my approval. When it all shakes down, the Christian walk is between a person and God, and my endorsement is neither required nor welcomed.

- I have been a Christian for 52 years, and I find it a regular source of amazement that a decision made as sincerely as a seven-year-old can make one is still valid today. I understand that it is not my intellect, age, or behavior that makes it true; it is the constancy of God. Nonetheless, it is a wondrous component of faith in Christ to me and, I suspect, to other believers as well.

- It is important to study not merely the English version of the Scriptures, but the texts and backgrounds of the words and situations. I do believe that the Bible is inerrant, and I believe that Jesus "is the same yesterday, today, and forever." But the Scripture was written for the people of that time too, with customs and places and events as part of it. So, I find great joy in researching passages of Scripture -- finding out the meanings behind the parables and the traditions of the writers and scribes. It helps me so much to learn about that world and makes the Word more alive in my imagination.

- If pressed about it, I would say that denominational choice is much more about personality and practice than about theology. That is not, of course, ironclad nor is it supported by empirical data (the scripture of our age), but I see examples of this all around. Extroverted people seem much more comfortable in churches with clapping and shouting than my introverted friends. To the first group, my home Presbyterian service would seem like a gathering of the frozen chosen, whereas those same Presbyterians would be appalled at the disorder of "Amen!" and standing up with arms raised. My disclaimer would be that theology is crucial, but these other factors impact heavily as well, and we Christians ought to be willing to admit it.

- Christians have to give people permission to be wrong and make mistakes without withdrawing the love and concern we are commanded to disperse. Why would non-Christians act or live as if they were Christians? It can't be done; without the indwelling of the Holy Spirit, we Christians would be as rudderless. So, while there are things I don't want to put into my rapidly deteriorating mind and places I don't want to go, I can't hold my help and love hostage from unbelievers unless they live as I do. "Love one another" isn't limited to other Christians, and we need to get off our sofas and stop congratulating ourselves on our salvation as if it were something we designed.

- "WWJD" is not the consummate end of Christianity, but rather a reminder of what I pray for God to manifest in my life. Some call it the exchanged life---asking God to live His life through me, rather than me attempting a stand-up imitation of Jesus. Frequently my prayers say things like, "Lord, either change my attitude or kill this person. I don't care which!" Nice, right? My point is that unless Christ gives me peace, I have none. Unless He gives me His words to say, I babble. So, daily I find myself saying, "Lord, where are You in the midst of this? What do I do?" And He regularly reminds me of things or calms my volcanic temper or floods my heart with peace when my insides feel like a washing machine agitator.

- All Christians don't have to agree on every single aspect of the faith. Of course, I think everyone should agree with me, but most humans are egocentric, aren't we? I certainly believe in eternal security and could argue it, but why? Prayer is the appropriate response, I think, to disagreements between Christians. I don't always act on that belief in the heat of the moment, but I do apologize for bad behavior when I mess up in this area. We have to give the Holy Spirit time to work in others' lives just as we hope for that same grace for ourselves. Maybe it is because I'm not a big arguer. I enjoy debate or spirited discussion but just briefly. Maybe I'm a wuss.

- Balance is the most elusive attribute of the Christian walk, I think. We get enthusiastic about something (tithing, witnessing, feeding the poor), and other equally important issues fall away. All of us can't do everything, but that imbalance is a reminder of the effect of sin on the world. For example, I am an extroverted, live-in-the-moment, emotion-driven person. That's how God made me. I need to accept Him and, on rare days of spirituality, thank Him for it. On the other hand, I need to learn to be quiet sometimes, not saying whatever comes into my head the minute I think it. I need to ask God to give me His balance because mine is often inexistent. So, I pray for balance often.

I'll stop for now. Write to me immediately, albeit as kindly as possible, if you want me to shut up for a while. I am not trying to kill either of us; in fact, I love you...me, only sometime.

Mrs. Z

The Blind Thing

The whole issue of losing the vision was not in one fell swoop but rather in small increments. It took a while to get to the legally blind stage, and it took a while to get some sort of diagnosis and prognosis. My perpetual state of oblivion worked well for me here, because I never really felt terror or horror or any sort of dramatic emotion at this stage. It was just sort of taking each day as it came.

As far as the school thing, that was a concern because I didn't know how I'd take care of Claire, nor if she'd have to leave her school and go to public school. The superintendent allowed me to teach just two classes a day, while retaining all of the benefits of a full-time teacher. As the vision got worse, the folks from the Department for the Visually Handicapped came in to see each class and show the equipment and talk about vision. These counselors did a lot of problem solving for me as well and paid for many supplies such as a large dry erase board to be mounted over the chalkboard. You see, I couldn't see what I'd written in chalk on the regular board, but using colored markers worked much better.

Counselors from DVH provided the reading machine,

which has some other real name, but I can't remember it. This thing, about the size of an overhead projector, had a moving platform on the base, a top that could be adjusted up and down for clarity, and a system of mirrors that threw the page I put on the platform up onto a screen. The screen could be adjusted as to angle, as well as whether the screen was white and the letters black or vice versa.

Therefore, I could put a book on the machine and read it without having to hold the book up to my nose. A student built a sort of riser for the podium that allowed the literature book or whatever I needed to read to be raised about six inches. That was invaluable, since lit books weigh a ton. The sides of the riser folded in, and there was a handle so that I could take it whenever I had to speak somewhere.

The glasses were, of course, the primary equipment for me. The Commonwealth paid for them, since I was not making the big money, and at $2100 and $3400 respectively, it was a good thing. The glasses that I used most of the time were tinted and had little tiny binoculars installed in each lens. That way if I wanted to see something far away, like on a grocery shelf, I could look through the tiny hole and see. The field of vision using the binoculars was very small, but it was helpful. The reading glasses were just like the loupes you see surgeons wearing, but I rarely used them. It was easier just to remove the glasses and read with the naked eye.

The DVH also provided me with a special radio that gets only the network in our area where volunteers read newspapers and magazines. There was a set schedule so you could plan to listen to whatever happened to appeal to you, and I enjoyed that. Of course, I listened to a zillion books on tape, which was a somewhat more sensitive system than just regular tape player and tapes. And don't let me forget the collapsible cane, which was quite a source of security for me, in that I could avoid falling down and threaten passers-by as needed. Another great thing found were checks which were not only larger, but had the lines embossed so that I could feel them and, using a felt-tip pen, I could write checks in a more normal posture.

The biggest problems for me were the loss of independence and the eye fatigue. It was hard to have to ask for help so often, and yet I had this unnatural fear (which I never overcame) of trying to take the bus. The frustration came when I couldn't go somewhere, or when the friend with whom I was going took much longer than had been projected. The worst thing that happened in that department was the day Claire and I got all dressed up for an important wedding and our ride forgot us. My fury was tremendous over that. Light bothered my eyes, so I wore hats when I taught and in church. One day, early into this hat-in-church thing, a stranger came up behind me and said that my plain hats were boring to those behind me, so if I would bring her my hats, she'd decorate them---and she did! What a blessing! I couldn't stand lamps on for long, so former student Brad came over and, after knocking down a big hornet's nest for me, strung up those little white Christmas lights around my crown molding. It was marvelous.

I believe that we do teach people how to treat us, and I generally want to be in charge, taking care of things and people. Those four years were so precious to me as the most intense time of being taken care of and shown such obvious displays of love. I could go on and on, but I'll just hit the high points.

After teaching my two classes, I'd change clothes and walk home, about a mile. I had this great visor, which I needed in addition to the big honking glasses to protect my eyes. The visor was great because it was covered with glitter and probably sent messages overseas with its brightness. So, I'd head out with my book bag and my gym bag with my clothes; I'd gotten to the point of not taking a purse, because with the backpack on my back, the gym bag in one hand and the cane in the other, a purse was too annoying. A couple of times as I walked home, I encountered some minor construction on the sidewalks, and both times someone guided me along with their voice. When a rain shower suddenly erupted, I broke my mother Frances' rule and accepted a ride with a lady in a little truck. I figured I could take her if she got smart with me!

The fourth-grade class held, completely unbeknownst to me, a bake sale to help me and donated almost $300 to me. Part of that money I used to buy a large print dictionary and thesaurus and a subscription to large print Reader's Digest. The mom of two former students volunteered to pick me up each Friday morning to take me anywhere I wanted to go to run errands. That was heaven, because being alone all day was very boring and lonely, and besides, their generosity made me more independent.

One thing I forgot to mention was that at the beginning of my odyssey into the world of low vision, I had sought assistance from DVR. At that particular time the department had a vision deficit requirement, which I had not yet reached, (I would later reach and exceed it, being the overachiever that

Ordered Steps

I am), though my vision was pretty bad. Since it was an agency requirement, I couldn't get the computer and glasses that I needed, and I was in a fix. Therefore, I contacted the Department of Rehabilitative Services to see if they would help me. The person with whom I spoke very patiently and in words of no more than two syllables informed me that since I already had a job, they couldn't help me. However, if I lost my job, then they could help me find a job. I mulled that over for a few days, becoming increasingly distressed that, as a taxpayer, I was paying people to lose their jobs so that this agency could find them new ones. I wrote to them.

Secretary Kay Coles James and I laid out my concerns about this inefficient and frustrating situation. I was polite but suggested that the wisdom of requiring me to become unemployed before I could be assisted wasn't all that wise. Her response was swift and sure, and I received a nice phone call from DRS offering to assist me. Mercifully, in the midst of that brouhaha, DVH had loosened the standards for visual impairment, and I could work with them.

I also had to apply for disability benefits, since I was working so little, and there is a six-month waiting period before you get any money. I would imagine that would be to ensure that the client has not received a healing of some sort. Now understand, that isn't six months to process the claim; that is six months after being approved. So, things were exciting at my house. In the midst of this, Frances pointed out to me that Claire's teeth were going in all directions, practically growing out of the palms of her hands. I got a referral to Dr. Richardson, thinking that I'd see what was needed and then work from there. When we went, he allowed as how she really needed braces yesterday and the total would be around $3200. I explained about my vision (while wearing these huge sunglasses against the fluorescent lights in his office) and stated that once the disability kicked in, I'd be back. I believe I said something like, "These days I'm praying in the groceries," and then he said, "Well, she really needs these, so we'll take care of it." With that, this delightful guy did a whole mouthful of braces and all the follow-up care for free! How cool is that!

I have all my blind stuff stored, because sometimes I've done presentations about teaching the handicapped, and sometimes (like last year) I take the stuff in to educate my kids. I had forgotten that, along with the cane and glasses and special checks, I had these two tee shirts that I used to wear with my warm-ups that were pretty funny. Both were printed in this wavy, unfocused font, and one said, "We walk by faith, not by sight." I've now, of course, forgotten what the other one said, but the kids would crack up.

I should also add to the list of kindnesses that Wendy, my hairdresser (hard to believe that my 'do would require such services, isn't it?), would come to my house to cut my hair. Some folks wouldn't think that was much, but it spelled love to me.

I should probably mention that my eye care, including surgery, was pretty much gratis. My doctors would write off anything not covered by my insurance, and so here came another gift of love. When I was healed, the eye tech gave me a frame for my new glasses (which I'm still wearing).

I should probably talk about the healing part. I was

diagnosed, at a regular checkup, as having grown cataracts along with the myopic degeneration (the final diagnosis). I guess when you find what you're good at, you should stick with it, and eye rot was definitely mine. I had the first cataract surgery and immediately noticed that everything was whiter and less golden. The second surgery was two weeks later, and with both of the eyeballs fixed, even without proper glasses, I knew that I could see. When I went to see Darin, my surgeon, for the first checkup after the surgery, I said to him as he stood staring at my file, "Okay, show me on that chart (anatomy of an eye) the reason that I can see. Not that I'm complaining, of course, but how come?" He shook his head slowly and said, "There is no reason that you should be able to see. God healed you." Everyone in this large office was stunned and so kindly thrilled for me, and when I got the license back (which required me to be tutored by Claire, who enjoyed this far more than was necessary) and a car, I gave Darin a framed picture of my license plate which said (and still does), "I CAN C." These days I enjoy explaining to the curious who ask about the plate, telling them, along with the blind man who met Jesus, "Once I was blind, but now I can see."

What was going on inside during all of this? Think I've spoken of boredom and loneliness sometimes, and of feeling dependent. Some days these things chased me around the house, and other days were fine. I remember being shocked when my sister Beth commented one time, "Don't know how you can stand it. If this happened to me, I'd have to 'off' myself." It didn't seem to me all that bad. Out of no sense of hyper-spirituality at all (just ask Claire how spiritual I wasn't some days), I never thought to pray to be healed. I figured that things happen, and my walk with the Lord wasn't altered because I was blind. You take what comes, pray like crazy, and do the best you can. A former friend became quite angry with me for not begging God to heal me, and while I'm not a big fan of conflict, I had to get real firm with her. I remember telling her that I belonged (and still do) to God and He gets to do with me what He will. It was His business, not mine, and while I'd be glad to see doctors and have help, it was just what my life had for me. No martyrdom here, dearie; just reporting the facts.

A couple of years ago a younger colleague (athlete, middle 30's, two sons) began to be quite ill with nothing that could be named. She was in pain and ill in so many ways, and she struggled to keep going. I wrote her a note, hoping to encourage her, and in the writing of it, some of my thoughts about my foray into sickness hardened. I wrote of all that had come my way in support and kindness and growth of character, and in closing said what I'd never realized until that moment. While I like seeing clouds and stars (I missed the stars so much when I was blind), I'd be blind again in a minute if God allowed it to happen, just to walk with Him and some of His children in the same way. As I write this, it is still true. The lessons that I learned and the love I was shown far outpaced any inconveniences I might have experienced, and mostly I learned that He is still my Father and He is still able.

Changed for the Better

In the first grade I had my mouth taped shut because I talked too much. Now, before calling Child Protective Services, remember that in those days life looked very different than it does these days. Back then teachers expected children to behave and, in most cases, we did. In my mother's words -- words which still resonate in my memory -- "You don't have to be the smartest child in your class, but you CAN be quiet!" And that was that. I should add that the teacher had called my mother during school, and the two of them talked the situation over. No more taping of the mouth for this girl!

It is pretty safe to say that life has changed quite a bit since that dark day, and I've still found myself in a classroom many a time. Twenty-eight years of teaching are behind me now, and while my dreams are frequently of classrooms and students, I find myself floating in a giant lake of free time, awash in memories of former students and events of the past.

The six years that I spent teaching at a juvenile detention facility and the students I met there are often on my mind these days. Friendships with staff still at the Center are probably partly involved in keeping those memories alive as we often do that do-you-remember-that-guy? and I'll-never- forget-the-time reminiscence.

Jamel was 14 with a girlfriend and a baby and the gift/curse of leadership and creativity in his "business." His business was drugs and leading a platoon of followers, and he was good at it. Blessed with a strong sense of himself and adept in getting people to follow him unquestioningly, he commanded his troops via a labyrinth of family visits (all females) and messages to other inmates to pass along through others in his army. I never heard him raise his voice or demonstrate any sort of bullying, but in that world, he was the king.

Jamel also possessed a quick intellect in the academics and quickly passed the GED test. His time at the D-Home (as referred to by the students) was coming to an end, and an idea popped into my mind one day. I asked him if he'd like to take an online college class, and his face was a mixture of what's-going-on-with-Mrs.-Z and his perpetually cool façade. "For real?" was his answer, and when I responded, "Yes, what do you think?" he replied, "Sure, why not?" Unexpectedly, his release came almost instantly, ending that possibility for Jamel, and I never saw him again. I heard through the street grapevine that he has moved his "business" to North Carolina, but his leadership, daring, and people skills keep his legend alive.

I also remember the reaction of another inmate who had overheard that conversation with Jamel regarding taking a college class. "Hey, Mrs. Z," one of the quieter, less colorful students had said one day. "You were going to pay for him to take a college class? How come?" Trying to play it off as that-was- then-this-is-now, I said, "Well, I had all this money sitting around and needed to get rid of it." Refusing to be dissuaded, he persisted, "You were going to pay for him to take a college class? Why would you do this? You work here; I know you ain't rich." After thinking for a moment or two, I told the boy the bare-bones truth. "I wanted him to see a different slice of the world, something he could be a part of that was totally unlike anything he'd ever seen or done. Also, I wanted him to know that he could do so much more with his life." The boy returned to his table, his expression one of thoughtfulness. I hoped that perhaps this boy might've heard something that made him think. For the rest of my years, the boy never returned.

Very rarely someone would show up in my class whose appearance demanded, "What in the world is he doing here?" His name was Gage, this boy with dark hair and downcast brown eyes. He spoke rarely -- most in a murmur -- and he never ever looked into anyone's eyes. From information from the staff and the few words he let me hear, I discovered that his mom was his only family, and she was sick. He was always assigned to a table alone because of his regular look of terror and sorrow. I'd sit down in the empty chair at his table and lean in to hear his faltering phrases. Out of the blue one day he said to me, "Would you put your hand on my arm?" A simple enough request, right? Wrong. There are strict rules regarding staff and inmate interactions, and the televisions from every room in the facility are watched and recorded. And yet, as I looked at this fragile, dejected boy of about fourteen years old, all I saw before me was a boy who missed his mother's touch, and so I put my hand on his forearm. In a moment his free hand covered mine, and we sat there silently for a minute or two. Then class was over, and I walked over to the principal's office to tell her what had transpired. Trepidation danced around the edges of my heart as I prepared to face this person who regularly and heartily rebuked me for being "too emotional" about the students. Walking into her office and recounting the situation and the he-said/I-said parts, I waited for the inevitable rebuke, but it did not come. She affirmed the wisdom and timing and response and sent me speechless on my way. Such responses were few and far between during those days, but I was grateful for the respite on that day.

There were often surprises during the day-to-day activities in the various pods. Though the bulk of our male students were in the 14-17 age groups, sometimes we did get our ration of younger boys. The regular practice for the students was to assemble in the dayroom, a large room down from which the rooms/cells are located. In the dayroom the students can play games or use the telephone, and their meals are served there as well. Before each class the boys sit in chairs (generally in a two-line seating arrangement), waiting for the next teacher to arrive. After some general comments from the teacher of that hour, the students would be called one by one to enter and sit in an assigned seat. The assignments could be based on grade levels or on specific tasks in which the student would be engaged. One day a younger student, probably 11 or 12, was sitting in the front row in the day room. As I entered the room and began to greet the students, before I could give any instructions this young student put his right hand in a circle over his mouth and said, "Ooh, the feets is fresh!" All eyes went immediately to my new Nikes. The white lace-ups were peppered with decoupage pictures of $100 bills. Around the place where the leather met the sole was a shiny gold stripe, and the heel sported big gold stripes. Truthfully, the shoes came from China and were certainly knock-offs, but on that day in that big room of young men in trouble, all eyes were on my new shoes and fresh feets!

The classroom which generally held the older males was a basic rectangle, with windows down the side into the dayroom and a door and large window at the back. The tables had room for two students, though to get a table alone was considered a real luxury. This particular pod was primarily for older students, many of whom were long-time veterans of our hospitality. For reasons which escape me today, I had brought an ice cream cake for the guys; probably they had accomplished something noteworthy, but after all, ice cream is ice cream. I handed out the plates of ice cream cake, spoons, and napkins, and everyone checked out the other plates as compared to theirs. Such a large number of adolescent males in one room produced great surges of testosterone, and I'd been careful to cut equal squares. Just as I was about to say something like, "Well, enjoy yourselves," a fellow in the front said, "Shut up, man!"

We all froze, some with spoons loaded and heading for an open mouth. "What's going on?" I asked the older, muscled student while the nearest staff edged a bit closer. His answer stunned everyone when he said, "Man, we ain't prayed yet!" I responded, "Well, you want to pray?" He said, "Yeah," the other guys put their spoons down, bowed their heads, and an ardent blessing was delivered. After a robust "Amen!" filled the room, the guys attacked their ice cream cake with great focus while the adults watched all of this in wonder. These guys, capable of criminal activity and violence regularly, had chosen to bless the food first and then to enjoy their unexpected treat. As for the adults, we were schooled by incarcerated adolescents. My father would've said, "Who'd a-thunk it?"

A short hall leading to a fenced-in yard was a sort of closet/storage area on the right side. That was the site of the first-ever library in the detention center. Within that small area five shelves were affixed to the wall with places at the narrow end for magazines. Some books seemed magically to appear, a large and beautiful mural was painted, and suddenly it became apparent that we were going to have a library. Each pod had an assigned day of the week to come to the library, and the boys tentatively began to read. It was slow in the beginning, what with some of the uninterested muttering, "I ain't read no books!"

I began to cull books from my own shelves and to "encourage" friends to donate as well. Phone calls to friends and relatives produced boxes of books. As a small wave of momentum began to swell, I bought bookmarks. Yes, I said "bookmarks" and there were cool cars and motorcycles and beautiful ocean scenes and, before you could blink, books were what the kids talked about and wanted. Imagine that -- reading became cool in the D-Home!

My sister died of cancer during that time, and I received an inheritance of substance. All of this going on in my life -- the sadness in my heart mixed with the wonder of buying books --

came together in a whirlwind of purpose and possibility. We were going to teach students how to choose books that would open the whole world and show them what life could be, and we did! Rip and Jody were the most enthusiastic and quickest whizzes. After obtaining the necessary permissions and parameters, the two began to scan sites offering the kinds of books we wanted for our library. When the books came, other fellows learned how to process the boxes of books, carefully checking the books in each box with the list enclosed. Others helped to organize the books into categories like fiction and non-fiction and biography, and then the final touch -- the label on the spine. What an astonishing impact this process had on adolescents who had until then scorned the idea of reading, not to mention the energetic enthusiasm of the formerly pessimistic staff watching the energy and enthusiasm of the students.

Out of that largesse from my sister Beth came books that touched incarcerated teens who chose to read and discuss and debate and, most significantly, who grew from reading those books. We had competitions between the different pods to see which group could read the most pages (determined by a highly developed formula based on numbers of students). We had visitors from the community who came and read with the different groups of young people, and most importantly, there were teenagers signing up to reserve a book that was already checked out. It wasn't long until books were being "loved" into pieces, and so we bought more copies. A miracle had been accomplished -- our students loved to read. What else could be better?

So many boys and girls came through our facility during my time there, and still today another generation is moving in and out of that detention center as if on an endless conveyer belt. Working in a place like this has been compared to living in a pressure cooker, and I'd agree. Endless demands zap like laser beams unexpectedly into our adult lives, and every young person on the planet drags burdens of confusion and loss and yearning, and how in the world do mere mortals aid all these broken people? The only true and real answer in life is this: we all must know who we are and Whose we are. That alone is the foundation upon which our lives and works must be built, and then we have to show up every day in whatever place we have been assigned.

Sounds too hard? It isn't hard; it is impossible, but that's the best part. You see, when you and I stand on that Rock and carry out the assignments we've been given, we all have front-row seats to see the greatest gift of all: a life secured on that Foundation.

Chivalry in Camouflage

Going to the hardware store is nothing less than a journey into perdition for me. Of course, I am a '90's woman, wielding a hammer and pliers with confidence; however, the finer points of the genre elude me, and so my trip that Saturday morning was not without uncertainty.

I drove directly and without event to the hardware store in my town and repeated my rehearsed request several times to various young employees who passed me on to other equally young employees. "I need a half-sheet of half-inch plywood for shelves" finally yielded the location, and finding the indicated bin, I selected one piece of board based on nothing more than financial considerations. Hoisting the bulky slab of wood and acquiring numerous splinters in the process, I walked in what I hoped was a nonchalant manner to the cashier, paid the $12.05 and escaped.

I carried the plywood out to the parking lot and leaned it against my car while opening the hatch door. Manipulating the board sheet of wood, I tried to slide it into the back of my Ford. The plywood which had seemed a manageable size in the store now loomed large next to my compact car. It was an unbending two inches too wide, and so while the farmers two parking spaces down discussed world affairs and the Old Testament, I turned that plywood in every direction which I could think of, but it would not be cajoled. Several giggling children in a pick-up truck only added to my discouragement, and soon I realized that I would either have to buy a larger car or turn around and go back into that hardware store for help.

Reluctantly I headed back to the store with the uncooperative wood. En route, it came to me that perhaps the sheet could be cut into smaller pieces and thusly would cause no more problems. Proud of my problem-solving skills in this foreign world, I carried the board confidently back into the store and left it under the confused supervision of one of the young employees. All of those formerly eager salespeople had mysteriously disappeared, and so I walked up and down the aisles for quite a while until I located one lone man immersed in the task of sorting bolts. While I hated to interrupt such intense dedication, I needed his help, so I asked if there was someone who could cut up my large piece of plywood into smaller pieces. His blank stare discouraged me, but I repeated my question doggedly. Confidence in my bright solution faded as he recited, "We don't have nobody to cut nothing," and turned back to his bin of bolts.

I had already begun to try to think of another solution when a middle-aged man in a camouflage jacket and farm implement cap looked up from his examination of garden tools. Expressionlessly he asked me, "What do you need?" His expression never changed while I told him about the plywood that was bigger than my car, and then he matter-of-factly stated, "We'll get it for you."

Stumbling in my astonishment, I made oh-no-I-really-couldn't-impose sounds, but he had turned back to his shovels, the issue settled. His teenaged son asked me where I lived and I told him, all the while wondering whether I would be the victim of some agrarian serial killer. The young man and I walked outside to their pickup, the sheet of plywood hefted neatly on his shoulder. While we waited for his father, the boy described the school project that had brought them to the store that morning. Soon, the still-somber older man emerged from the hardware store and headed toward the glistening truck, so I turned insecurely to my car. As I pulled into my driveway, in my mirror I saw the truck stopping in front of my house. The son stepped out of the cab, pulled the plywood from the immaculate truck bed, and carried it wordless up the graveled driveway and onto my porch while I thanked him profusely. He completed his delivery, said simply, "You're welcome," walked back to the truck and climbed in. I waved vigorously at their backs and then walked into the kitchen, still puzzling over the events of that Saturday morning.

What is so amazing about one person helping another person? Well, it seems to me that chivalry far too frequently is motivated in social situations by the hope of reciprocity. No, all men aren't rude any more than all women are helpless, but the rush of life, the preoccupation with success, and even the fear of the unknown have made folks unprepared for the unexpected kindness of a stranger. In too many neighborhoods if a stranger offers to deliver something for you, too often you can plan on losing that item or perhaps even your television later. Here in

Radford on a Saturday morning, however, chivalry wore camouflage, and the knight drove a red pickup truck.

Christmas in our Barn

The Christmas tree was mangy and leaned dangerously to the right. I tried turning the leaning side back toward the wall, but that looked awful too. Finally, I used fishing line to lash the tree to some nails in the wall and stood back to view the results. It wasn't great, but with just the tree lights on, it was definitely Christmas.

On the phone with friends that night, which ones I can't exactly remember, I must've talked a lot about how hard it is being divorced and on a small income. Since it was a school night, soon I climbed the stairs up to the large bedroom that I shared with my second grader. As I fell asleep, I prayed for the strength it always takes to teach during December.

After the kind of day which I had prayed not to have, I drove the 45 minutes home talking with my daughter about school, the upcoming Christmas program, and of course, The Big Day. We parked the car on the double driveway, noting that the owners of the home on whose property we lived were there, and walked down the sidewalk behind the pine trees to the barn-house we rented.

When we pushed open the screen door to the porch, I

noticed some sort of box out of the corner of my eye but kept walking the remaining two steps to the front door of the house. As soon as I opened the door and Claire followed me in, we saw that things weren't the same as we had left them that morning. Claire grabbed my coat and whispered, "Has the boogeyman been here, Mom?" I scanned the room quickly and then walked into the center of the large downstairs great room which served as the living room, dining room, and kitchen. Though Claire's eyes darted everywhere, her hand still hung on to my coat. Together we made a circuit around the room, touching each new thing.

You see, the boogeyman hadn't come at all. An anonymous someone had come into our trustingly unlocked home while we were at school and had delivered Christmas. There was a very tall, very straight, full-of-our-ornaments tree shining with more lights than we had ever owned. Our old rescue mission tree was in that box on the front porch.

Everywhere we looked there was some decoration or gift. Claire spotted the Christmas tree candy dish full of red and green M&Ms and stuffed some into her mouth. In the kitchen there were Christmas dishtowels, Santa Claus magnets on the refrigerator, and even salt and pepper shakers in the shapes of Santa and Mrs. Claus. By then all we could say over and over like a record with a stuck needle was, "Hey, come look at this!"

Christmas hand towels in the bathroom, red ribbons up the stairs to the bedroom, a music box on the table between our beds, even Christmas stationary tucked into the desk drawer beside the bills. Everywhere we looked there was Christmas and there was an unknown friend. I was still a single parent, there were still bills to be paid, and the vagaries of life were still out there waiting for us, but right here, right now, there was magic.

In the years which have passed since then, Claire and I have talked about that day. Claire's memories are of lights and surprises and something to talk about in show-and-tell at school. Mine are of faithful friends and a faithful Father teamed up in a celestial tag-team match for my soul. That's who I always want in my corner.

Nancy Wade Zappulla

Don't Forget the End Game

Funny how we can get an idea stuck in our minds, isn't it? A random phrase, a short conversation – even just a few words can tunnel themselves into our brains and voila! They're stuck forever in concrete. Strange how ideas put down roots in our memories and instantly become fact – how it really was. Well, let me give you an example from my own life.

One Saturday when I was about $13\frac{1}{2}$ (that one-half being of great import), I was hanging out clothes. After an eternity, the hated task was over, and freedom was mine. Before I could get to the back door, Mom stepped out and began to talk about a phone call from the pastor about a camp for underprivileged kids needing help and what a good thing it would be for me to help them. Couldn't say no to that, could I? More details escaped my memory but...

And the rest is history. The next ten or so summers saw me working at this camp in a variety of assignments. I worked in the kitchen, taught Bible during girls' weeks, taught basic horseback riding, and even was assistant director of the girls' camping weeks, discipling the female staff.

And I lived happily ever after. THE END.

Ordered Steps

But you know, and I know that life in general and the spiritual life in particular is never that simple. We humans are much more complicated than all that, and life is never, ever that simple.

So-o-o what really happened? I'll tell you, but we'll have to go back to the place it all began and all of the folks who were there.

I was assigned to work in the kitchen since I was too young to work with the campers. I did whatever tasks I was assigned before and after the meals and also waited tables during the meals. Outside of work time, we girls of the kitchen world lived in "The Dormitory," a concrete block building with one huge space for beds and suitcases and another room with a charm of its own. The bathroom was split into a 2/3, 1/3 arrangement. The larger room sported three toilets side by side facing three sinks directly across the opposite wall. The other third was a gang shower featuring a shower head on each wall and a wide opening of a door. These conveniences made for unending giggles, stories, and what could've been more fun?

Well, I'll tell you what could've been more fun, but first a bit of the specifics of the kitchen/dining hall structure. The large metal building, often having been used in military installations, was used for a myriad of storage and work requirements. Imagine a gigantic metal tube cut in half and plopped on a large field. The open ends were covered with screens and closed with large sliding doors. Unless the rains were torrential and pouring directly at the screened ends, the doors stayed open. Over the kitchen area was a loft where the maintenance guys slept and piled up mountains of clothes of dubious cleanliness.

The kitchen operated with at least two and sometimes three stalwart grown-ups on duty. They planned the menus, stocked the large pantry adjacent to the kitchen, and generally ran the whole operation. Feeding a herd of kids three times a day was at best a long-distance race and, at worst, mayhem.

You see, the campers came on Sunday afternoon and left on the next Saturday morning but not nearly quickly enough, thought the exhausted staff. Their weekends were spent dumping mounds of laundry somewhere near the family washing machine, showering, eating, sleeping, and packing to return after church on Sunday afternoon. Makes you wonder who was more exhausted after this weekend regime, doesn't it?

So, staffing was determined by whether it was boys' week (girls only in the kitchen) or girls' week (only boys doing maintenance and working with the horses). Between this mass of hormone-saturated adolescent staff stood the Director and other adults who did everything else a camp would need. These were the hardy, ever-vigilant, ever-diligent folks who even now are recuperating from that ministry to which they were assigned. And not much money was passed around either. We were doing it "as unto the Lord." Within this ever-changing, ever- pulsating landscape of children, teens, and adults, we sought and found friends and mentors and (dared we breath it?) love. But that's a story for another time.

The two girls with whom I spent the most time and knew the best were Carol and Daisy. Carol and I went to the same church, and our families enjoyed regular get-togethers. Plus, she was two years older, which was a big deal at that age. I met

Ordered Steps

Daisy at camp, and she quickly became the star of the kitchen. An efficient and quick learner, she focused on the tasks and completed them swiftly and successfully. She and I laughed incessantly, performing in "The Flash-light Follies" in the dormitory to screams of laughter.

And yet I realized that while our friendships were strong and sure, these two friends excelled in areas of struggle for me. I didn't know as much or have as much experience in the kitchen and fumbled my way through many a meal. Daisy was efficient, focused, and successful. Carol had leadership jobs which she undertook with unflappable confidence and regular success. Having worked at another camp, she brought new ideas to our camp. I wasn't jealous (often); mostly, I'd have described myself as "inept" if I'd known the definition of that word. In the mirror I saw someone who just wasn't catching on as quickly or efficiently as Daisy did, nor was I as proficient as Carol was. Among the three of us, we felt pretty equal, but in the sight of those adults who supervised us, I saw myself as a back-of-the-field third who never caught up. Now, lest you imagine that I was a wallflower, I yucked it up and had lots of fun with the campers and other staff. It was during my down times of life I thought I'm-never-gonna-be-as-good-as.... In my heart I was a sloppy third.

And life went on, and people grew up and/or old or all of the above, and God has shown Himself faithful to us all along in so many ways. Carol and Daisy and I have been friends for eons, our lives woven through each another's. The adults of influence have also filled their lives with families and ministries, and all of us have seen God stretch our lives and faith-walks. Looking at us, we've turned out reasonably well, I'd say. My daddy would have said we've been copacetic, a word from the '40's meaning "doing just fine."

So, what happened to me, the sloppy third? God showed up on this particular issue just a few weeks ago, obliterating that old wound in a most unexpected fashion. Here's what happened.

I'm still involved with people and aspects of Hope Haven. In the interim years Hope Haven has provided homes for children from distressed family situations as well as care for senior adults. I had the opportunity to work in both of those aspects in my thirties, and many of those adults from HH days were working there as well. During those years my father was elected to be on the Board of Directors of the Union Mission, Inc., which is the parent ministry from which was born the other helping ministries. I keep in touch with both those who supervised me as well as those with whom I worked. They learned a long time ago that they can run, but they cannot hide.

Recently Mrs. Bashford went to heaven, and an era ended. She and her husband had poured their lives into making all of the ministries of the Union Mission the powerful influence for good that they are today. Surprised, I cried more than usual at the news of her home-going and began to figure how to get to Tidewater for the funeral.

You see, I can't drive anymore and live in Lynchburg, from which no public transportation has a direct route to that area. Speaking with Linda Vaughan (Bashford daughter #3, most recently director of the ministry), I explained my obstacles and reiterated my intense desire to be there. She strongly encouraged me to come, and I commenced to bombard heaven with my prayers. Imagine my surprise when my friend Lisa called to ask if I'd like to get a ride with her to Virginia Beach.   She was going to visit friends there and knew I've always been ready for a trip "home." I hung up and pulled my suitcase out immediately.

The entire weekend was flooded with a golden glow. Visiting with my-friend-since-8th-grade Polly always means big fun, and the time with other old friends is always both a treat and frequently a surprise. Polly drove me down to N. Landing Road, the site upon which Camp Hope Haven has always had camp as well as residences for needy folks, saying, "Just call me when you're ready for me to come." I tried my best not to fall down in my good clothes – even wore girl shoes rather than my favorite Vans.

When I opened the door, I saw a cavernous space with several large round tables. I stopped and just stood there, trying to get my bearings. Without any warning I heard the sound of a woman squealing, "Nancy!" and here she came with her arms stretched straight out, running toward me. It was Marie, a lady from my home church, and that was just the beginning. For more than an hour I saw friends from my home church, the Bashford clans, "kids" who had worked at camp and were kids no longer. Even one of my students from Portsmouth Christian Academy was there! It was an all-encompassing time in that familiar place, and many hours have been spent remembering and crying just a little bit and talking again with folks I saw there. I kept thinking, "Lord, this is what heaven will be like, seeing all of these folks I've loved."

Several days later a conversation with Linda which started out pretty ordinary turned life-changing for this kitchen helper of fifty-five years ago. Thanking Linda yet again for inviting me, her answer went something like, "Well, Aunt Nancy, I wanted you to be here. It was important to me that you came." Simple words, right? But into my ears and heart, God poured through Linda words which silences all those years of feeling less than and not enough. Remember, no one had ever said those negative words to me, but through the years they had sounded like a repeating bell in my head and heart. Now, with Linda's words resonating in my memory, my loving Father has banished them.

Some things don't change, like surgeries and confusion and loneliness. Some things last forever like forgiveness and love and joy, and this story. Oh, this one I'll never stop telling. In my home church we sing a song that says, "He may not come when you want Him, but He's always right on time!" And He is, He really is. God's gift of Linda's words wiped all those old sorrows away, and that weight has been lifted. And God taught me (and I suspect this is for you as well) that no matter how long the struggle may last, He always has an end game. We just have to watch for it.

First Library

I remember the first library I ever saw. My mother piled the three of us kids – I was the oldest, then Beth, then Ricky – into the 1952 Chevrolet, drove for what seemed like forever, and finally parked next to a square, gray stone building.

I was in first or second grade at the time, and to me, the library looked like a skyscraper. When we walked through the doors, I remember that it had a special smell that I've never forgotten. The brown wooden half-circle desk was directly in front of the door with its back to the far wall. The two ladies who stamped books and answered questions had gray hair piled on the tops of their heads, and I was never afraid to talk to them. That they had said the same things and answered the same questions to countless other children never occurred to me, and I thought of them as a sort of civilian Santa Claus, dispensing wonderful treasures and softly spoken kindnesses to me each time I approached them.

Grown-up books were on the right, and our books on the left. The windows went right up to the ceiling without curtains, and the shelves ran along the walls under those big windows. I remember that I had to turn my head sideways to read the titles on the spines of the books, and when I found some books I wanted to check out, I could sit at the shiny wooden tables. As the oldest, I was supposed to help the younger ones. I'm not sure how I managed to evade that task at the library, but every once in a while I escaped. I just sat by my pile of books while the others finished their searches until it was time to go. Sometimes when I read my books and I thought no one was watching, I'd stick my nose into the pages and smell the old paper and ink fragrance that assured me these were very old and valuable books, full of magic.

There were always libraries at the various schools I attended, and our parents were avid readers as well. That meant trips to libraries were regular, and a new book by a favorite author was a treat well-appreciated in our family. So, I grew up in and out of libraries, learning by example and experience that answers to questions of all sorts could be found there. Family discussions were often ended by Dad's favorite statement, "Go look it up," and we knew just where to go.

Navigating the university library for graduate studies was a daunting experience for me, a newly turned 40-year-old. There were several official-looking desks in that library, often in the same room, and intricate instructions were posted regarding which questions could be directed to whom. Though my university library was large and boasted many computers and microfiche machines and probably other gadgets I never discovered, its redemptive qualities for me were several.

First, despite copy rooms and audio-visual labs, this library had large shiny wooden tables with straight-back wooden chairs. Though the gloss on the tables was often scarred by the scraping of all of those notebooks and pens, the tables were still large enough to stack piles of books I might check out without crowding others at the tables. Unlike most other surfaces in the university, there was no graffiti carved into these tables. I could open reference books and take notes and make little piles around me, and the table supported all my labor.

The library also had, as well, the official library smell. The thousands of books being opened and shut on of the floors had allowed the fragrance of old books to permeate the library. I suppose if someone worked there for any period of time or if they had never known that odor before, it went unnoticed. I noticed it, however, the first day that I arrived, and it felt like a homecoming of sorts as I pushed through the swinging leather-covered doors by the circulation desk. Every once in a while, buried far back into the stacks, I'd pull down some old journal or rebound book, open it randomly, and inhale the official library smell. It helped me to focus better somehow. Those university librarians looked different than the sweet old ladies of my youth. There were so many staff in that cavernous building, and they had different titles, and I was often stymied as to whom I should address my multiplying questions. I solved that dilemma quickly by selecting those librarians who came from behind their fortress desks and walked with the seeking student. The reference librarians walked miles round that first floor and displayed Job's patience in repeating the same instructions regarding the computers, hour after hour. Their patience and resourcefulness provided support as tangible as their tables. One of them, the mysterious Bud, searched libraries across the country for articles I needed, his turquoise-bedecked hands busy with reference guides and fax machine. I remember thanking him in a particularly profuse fashion after he had obtained a large stack of materials I needed, and for free too. He dipped his bearded head and thanked me for keeping him valuable, and therefore employed. The publication of my first article using that information sent me to dial his number right after my mother's, and he was part of that celebration.

These days I go to the library less frequently. Time and the circumstances of my life restrict me somewhat, but whenever I venture inside, there are still the wide wooden tables, the ladies to answer my questions, and most of all, the magic of what can be.

The Football Player and the Middle-Schooler

For the almost one-and-a-half years of my relationship with Jonathan, he has been skirting disaster. He was my student as a sophomore, and while he found managing his personal effects more than a little overwhelming, he had a huge heart which he would cover with extremely intricate maneuvers. I remember one day that the class -- first period it was -- decided that it was time to rearrange the room. Changing things around was a commonplace event in my class, but I usually did it during lunch or after school. For some reason, however, on that morning we began to brainstorm on a new set-up. We tried different designs, but the bell rang before we could complete our experimental arrangement. I remember Jonathan taking an unusually intense interest and part in this project, and long after the bell rang, he was still talking and moving chairs. Another time I had given some lengthy assignment to be turned in on a Friday. The class raised some objections at the last minute, citing huge projects in other classes, and so I agreed to put off the due date until Monday. Usually one of the last to leave the room, Jonathan turned to me and said, "Mrs. Zappulla, moving that day will mess you up, huh? I bet you were gonna use the weekend to correct those papers and now you can't." Then he was out in the hall, yelling at someone or yanking some girl's purse off her shoulder, while I stared after him, amazed. At the end of the year, I told him that I believed that he would grow up to be a terrific husband and father because he has such a tender heart and an eye for details. He looked at me without blinking and replied, "Oh yeah? You really think that about me?" and was gone again.

But that was last year and now Jonathan is a mighty junior and a football player. I don't teach his English section, and so our contact is irregular. I hear about him, however, since he spends much time in the office discussing his problems with the dress code. Specifically, Jonathan has a hip problem: he has none upon which to hang his pants, and so they are always falling far below the acceptable site, as defined by both the school board and polite society. Whenever I see him, I try to ask about life and such niceties before launching into what I hope is a concerned comment about his behavior record. Often, I fear that I fail, and rather than loving concern, Jonathan hears yet another adult scolding him.

Jonathan's name comes up frequently at home this year also. My middle-school daughter has mentioned him in our morning prayers faithfully since school began. Wondering why it is Jonathan out of so many high schoolers for whom Claire is praying, I asked her if he comes into my room while I'm at devotions or if she talks to him. Such a question could evidently only be answered with a look of incredulity and polysyllabic, emphatic "No-o!" Why then does she pray for him morning after morning at 7:00 a.m., long before I'm coherent enough to remember the names of my students? When asked this hopefully less insulting question, she shook her head and replied, "I dunno. I guess God just put him in my head."

Last week, after an early morning prayer had been offered on his behalf, Jonathan was once again in the office. When I came in and saw him sitting there, I began to half-tease, half-fuss at him. We joked a little as he assured me (for the zillionth time) that he hadn't done anything, and soon it would be straightened out. My parting shot to Jonathan, sent with less- than-loving motive, was "Jonathan, and to think that Claire prays for you every morning!" Before the office door swished shut, his voice slid through. "Tell her not to give up on me."

I wrestled with the searing truth of Jonathan's last minute as I returned to my room. This six-foot plus football player who is old enough to grow his own personal moustache and drive a moving vehicle wants the prayers of an eleven-year-old girl he'd probably never notice? Or was his comment merely some adolescent afterthought, designed to curry favor with a potential ally? Could it be that this young man, replete as he is with questions and missed cues and out-of-step behavior, is a child of God reaching out for the support of another child of God, not caring about artificial obstacles like age and gender and station? Knowing Jonathan, I cast my lot with the last suggestion, believing that the Holy Spirit works in his young life as well as in my daughter's and knowing that the God who put Jonathan in Claire's head is the same God who knows when a sparrow falls.

I just have to wonder how this unlikely pairing will end, this prayer partnership between two young people. What lessons will Jonathan and Claire learn as they pray and are prayed for? More importantly, what lessons are there for those of us more mature in years and faith? Would it have occurred to any of his teachers that Jonathan could be touched by the prayers of an eleven-year-old girl? Do we even pray for him, or do we merely try to survive him? God's words floated through that door to every other teacher: "Don't give up on me!"

Four Yellow Chairs

You carried four yellow chairs today. They must have weighed about 15 pounds; and you carried them about 40 feet. The entire process consumed, at best, about three minutes, and then you probably went on to something else. Maybe you helped with the children's activities or perhaps you went on to an evening worship. By the time you reached your destination, your mind was on something else, and those four yellow chairs were quite forgotten.

I, on the other hand, did not forget. What I remembered was that you carried the four yellow chairs. I had put them into my car to return them to church, and I drove up to the side door, planning to put them into the nearest classroom. Then you appeared and with the words, "Here, let me take those in for you." You made an impact on the life of my child and this single mom, too.

You see, we live in a world of just us two. We carry out the trash ourselves, we put things together with our little red toolbox in hand, and we open our own doors. It's not necessarily our choice, but it is our life. I guess we're accustomed to "hoeing our own row," as my grandmother used to say.

So, in the midst of our handle-it-ourselves world, you helped us carry four yellow chairs, and you were the love of Christ to us. My young child asked me why you would help us when you don't even know us, and I was glad to be able to say, "Because he loves Jesus and wants to be kind." For her, carrying four yellow chairs said something about kindness and gentleness from a Christian man. For me it was the momentary respite from responsibility for every single aspect of life. It was respect paid to me as a woman and a picture of true manliness. I knew God cared about me more clearly that night.

You probably open doors and carry heavy loads regularly without thought, and it is doubtful we'll ever meet again. Know this, however, that your courteous gesture sent a beam of God's love streaming over us, and we thank you.

And all of this because you carried four yellow chairs.

A Friend Like Molly

She snuggled against me, eight-year-old legs tangled in a cartoon comforter. I lay on my back in her twin bed, a tousled brown head resting on my shoulder, sun-browned arms hugging mine. It was her favorite time, this just-before-sleep island of peace, and she had begged fervently for a talk.

"Please, Mom, just lay with me for a minute. We haven't talked in generations!"

Laughing, I agreed, defining her grown-up word as I rearranged all of the stuffed animals and moved the omnipresent cat to the foot of the bed. It promised to be a gentle, restful moment, and she was right. We hadn't done this for a long time

We settled down into comfortableness and listened to the hum of the air conditioner and one another's breathing. Abruptly she broke the hush. "Mom, why have so many hard things happened to me?"

Needing to catch my breath, I asked her to tell me more of her thoughts, and she did. She listed in minute detail the hurting parts of her life, and then she identified the empty places in her world that she saw filled up in her friends' lives.

I spent the next several minutes lining up the clearest explanations I knew for the year of unthinkable pain and loss that had been hers. I never lied about the hard parts, and I owned up to the parts that I didn't understand. She listened silently and then asked to go to the bathroom. I slipped out of her room.

I stared unseeingly at a television rerun and wept at everything on the screen. The poignant prematurity of my little one's question overwhelmed me, and the answers which I had given to reassure her now mocked me. Why should she have to wrestle with the ageless questions of suffering and justice when her playmates were unaware of pain beyond a stubbed toe? Over and over I reviewed the reasons I had recited for her, continuing to brush away endless tears. Each argument I had given her was based on the truth of my faith in Jesus Christ and His love for her, yet still the waves of anger and indignation surged over me. Pacing around my small living room, I chased peace, understanding and reconciliation between principles and emotions, faith and life. It was a race that I had to win.

Resolution crept in slowly and unnoticed at first. Faith which cannot be examined is no faith at all, and truth which is real Truth can stand any scrutiny. I could question and investigate, yes, and agonize, and both my faith and I would still survive. The Truth on which I had built my life -- God's love for and redemption of mankind in the person of Jesus – could not be destroyed by my painful experiences. My answers to my daughter that night would always be my answers; they would not change or disappear because the Truth on which they were based would not change.

I tiptoed into the dimly lit room and knelt by her bed. Her warm hand was open next to her face, and I pressed it to my cheek. May I be ready for the next question and the one after that and the one after that, I prayed. And may I always be honest with her questions and my answers. Rising to my feet, I tucked Molly the sock monkey under the covers beside her and watched my daughter hug her old friend tightly. Turning off her nightlight, I went to bed hugging my own comfort close.

Nancy Wade Zappulla

The Goblin Bee

But, now, uncertain of the length
Of this, that is between,
It goads me, like the Goblin Bee
That will not state its sting.
      -- Emily Dickinson

It's almost impossible to believe that it was forty-plus years ago – our time in that tiny northeastern town in Iowa. Back then I was never quite convinced that there really was such a place as Iowa. Nonetheless, the people and places and events and conversations in which we were submerged back then – the power of the time I spent there – I've just never forgotten any of it.

We were relatively newly-weds looking for what we'd do with our lives. I'd graduated from college and taught, and he'd worked in auto shops and facilities for special-needs folks. It was that desire to strike off, to go somewhere and do something unexpected, and that we surely did. With rapid-fire speed we filled out forms, rattled our ways through telephone interviews, and soon we were cramming that orange VW bug right up to the windows and heading for our great adventure.

The first thing I remember after three days was an A&W Root Beer drive-in, and I'd never seen such a thing. Then there were houses and more houses, but not like the three-versions-of-a-style house sort of neighborhood I'd grown up around. They were individually placed – some close to the road, some set to one side of the yard or another, some set back from the road – and, then I began to notice something strange to me. As we drove further into the little town, there were only white people. No black or brown people, no Asian folks – just white people who looked unblinkingly back at us. Not exactly weird, just different.

We somehow found a place to stay until a permanent place showed up, and then it was off to see Three Crosses Ranch. Nine hundred and fifty acres of rolling hills and blue skies with yards of clouds and a gravel road up to barns and sheds and a taller building with one-story building growing out of the middle. That was what we'd travelled three days to find, and it was beautiful and exciting in my eyes.

And life began. Husband would work with the older, more dedicated wrong-doer boys, while I would work with the rookies. The shifts were 7a-3p or 3p-11p. I'd spend the bulk of my time on the morning shift, which was made of breakfast, chores, and then activities (in the summer) or school for the rest of the day. My guys ranged in ages from 11-18 and were mostly from dreadful home lives full of negligent and mean-spirited or just absent adults. Two of them were quite a bit larger than I, but most of them were young guys still built more like children than teens.

Our first daily assignment was always the rabbits. Housed in a smallish building (as opposed to the huge barns), the rabbits were kept in wire cages with downward-slanting corrugated metal hung beneath. The boys had to put fresh water and some hay into each cage, brush the hanging metal clear of debris, and sweep up the aisles. It was repetitious and so-o-o boring from the boys' point of view, but as the program director explained, "These guys have had no routine in their chaotic lives, so this is one of the ways we teach them about routine and responsibility. These are foreign concepts to our guys, and they need to learn these skills," and he was spot on target.

Snippets of the lives of these fellows oozed or spewed out around the daily lives at the Ranch. One young guy who was one of five children (all in residential facilities) lived in a trailer where, during the summer, the mother would put a large wash pan of water on the porch for the kids, and then she'd lock the door. Another older boy was traded by his mother for a saddle for her horse. More than one of them had been a side-kick to the illegal activities of older relatives. And school? Who bothered with going to school? And, if you did go, you generally ignored school work. Billy stood out, not at all typical. He was a passionate reader, loving the great sagas of ancient and/or mythical heroes and villains, and he emerged from these worlds with reluctance. Patrick, a young guy who early on had to have his head shaved for smoking in the barn (a great transgression on a farm), redeemed himself when he reported that the silo holding the grain was getting hot to the touch. To this day I can't remember what that bode, but Patrick was heartily congratulated by kids and staff alike for saving that grain. His reward? A highly envied brand new five-dollar bill.

And I loved everything about the tiny town of Strawberry Point – the people who talked to everyone, the small rack of assorted blank bank checks from the surrounding four or five small towns ("just in case you forgot yours"), the gigantic strawberry on the tall pole in front of City Hall, the building just across from the big strawberry which featured a car wash/bowling alley/bar/restaurant, and the piercing shriek sounding at 6 p.m. nightly to alert the farmers in the fields. We didn't know it right away, but soon we discovered that we had joined a tribe of young married folks who had come to work at Three Crosses, and in these folks were born our first couple-friends. The Ranch was a Christian agency, and so we also shared our faith and the values which sprang from that faith.

We worked together, shared interests and talents, and found in our small town and the residents therein a place which quickly became home. Even the winters weren't daunting to me, full of new sorts of winter attire like snowmobile boots and one- piece coveralls and the like. I especially enjoyed the inserts to the boots. They seemed to have been made of felt (I wasn't sure), but this treasure not only kept my feet warm at -10 degrees outside but acted as great slippers. Especially enjoyable was the wondrous little wood stove we learned to cherish, and, couple these marvels with the new-to-me heated sidewalks, and I had no plans ever to leave.

And then Husband was dismissed, and we must pack and return to Virginia. Even now I remember so clearly those moments and days which followed, and how cheated I still feel even now after all of these many, many years later. But I didn't know then what I know now that this was just the beginning of thirty such firings and the upheavals that always tagged along.

Why? That's always the first question, whether in the swell of the storm or in retrospect. Why-did-I? Why-does-he? Why, why, why? These were not only the constant chorus in my head then but even now sometimes. I am comforted by the fleeting years because I can remember the encouragement from friends and family and the Bible and always, always, always the reminders inserted into my heart and head by my loving Father. You see, God never promised a pain-free life, but what He did promise was His presence, His Word, and His power. In those ensuing years of confusion and sorrow and lie after lie, there was my real life with God. My interminable conversations with Him (during which I'd frequently think, "He must get so tired of my whining!") which were then so unending have become just a little poke in my heart every now and then. No stabs, rarely tears, just a conversation with my Father, and my life moves straight ahead.

Now I know it was better for me, the not-knowing of the years ahead and the promise-breaking, law-breaking, heart-breaking barren desert over which my child and I would trek. Now I know it was better for me to live through those days and months and years. And right about now you're thinking, "What is wrong with this woman?" Some pseudo-intellect might intone, "Well, that was then, and this is now." And now – you want to hear about now, do you?

A hackneyed phrase – that was then, and this is now – contains the rest of this story. Life is life with its fits and starts, missed opportunities and mistaken beliefs, and most of all, the eternally present and eternally active God of all there is. And the humans of the story? Our family is, as my mom used to say, "percolating right along." God continues to work in our hearts and lives while teaching us to depend more and more on our Father God. Small as our family may be in number, our lives pulsate with the presence of Christ. And while we rejoice in our lives, always the bumps and unwelcomed surprises still show up with annoying regularity, just as everyone else experiences. And like everyone else, I don't love life's struggles, and yes, I do gripe. But then I gather together all those irritations and losses and those bad-old-day memories and recent wounds, and my Father and I talk about it. And you know what? He is God all by Himself. And I move along, strengthened by His love and courage, and well, you know, the percolating continues.

And to the Goblin Bee, I say, "Buzz off !

Nancy Wade Zappulla

God Comes to Dress Rehearsal

Unable to afford a ticket to the performance of the church Christmas musical, I slipped into the back row of the sanctuary during the Friday night dress rehearsal. Shrouded in near darkness and clothed in my weekend uniform of sweats and tennis shoes, I settled back and waited for the entertainment. That was what this whole program was about, as far as I could tell. After all, when you've been a "career Christian" as I have, saved young and working in various ministries, then you've heard all the songs. There aren't any surprises left.

I watched all of those faces which have in a short time become so familiar and dear, and I thought for the zillioneth time that in heaven I'd be able to sing like those folks on stage. I intentionally turned away from the weekly hashing-over of the previous week, full as it was of interruptions satanic, from small but annoying vehicular problems to impending financial doom. I was there to forget, to be entertained, to be infused with Christmas cheer.

It happened somewhere after the miniature pony number. A different message took over my attention, and the automatic foot-tapping to tunes I could sing in my sleep slowed and then stopped. I found myself listening to the narrator's words with an unexpected intensity. The song of the Three Kings awoke within me a yearning to lift my hands in praise right there in my dark pew. The jolt of "Emmanuel, God is with us" broke through a heart easily dulled by bills and dishes and papers to grade, and it was suddenly true for me. God was with me, and Christmas was genuine!

So, though the church will be full night after night and the songs will be repeated over and over and instruments will be packed and unpacked, for me the wonder has already taken place. God reached into that pew in the midst of all of the confusion of a rehearsal, lifted my limping spirit, and gave His gift to me -- the unmitigated joy of my salvation. Though the singers, the technicians, and musicians might have seen it as merely practice, for me it was the biggest night of all.

Nancy Wade Zappulla

Growing Up at Rices

Mrs. Fancher, Nancy Ipock, Mrs. Narducci, Mr. Marker...these were the names running through my mind as I read the clipping my mother had mailed to me. It was the obituary of Mr. Bishop, the manager of Rices, a department store in which I had worked during and after college. As I read about Mr. Bishop and his life, the pictures of that store and the people in it crowded into my thoughts.

I had first worked for Mr. Bishop during Christmas vacation of my freshman year of college. The gift wrap department was in the back left corner of the store, and a less creative gift wrapper than I never existed. My co-worker taught me three basic wraps, and I did those same three styles over and over during those two weeks of vacation. During my dinner breaks and infrequent free moments, I wandered through each area, making friends with the salesclerks and trying to look casual while computing the employee discount on things I liked. While it was my first experience at working all during Christmas vacation, I liked the early-morning freshness when I opened the department and the joyous let-down of finishing the final package and straightening up the cluttered giftwrap area at night That seasonal job began a lengthy association with Rices in my young adult years. During summers, vacations, and then into the early unsettled years of adulthood I could always count on a job somewhere in the store. I worked with Mrs. Hobson who tried desperately to teach me how to use the huge adding machine, I cashiered in ready-to-wear with Mrs. Fancher who never stopped smiling as I mis-rang numerous sales, and eventually would, with Mr. Bishop's recommendations, move to the main branch to work in the advertising and buying offices. That ended when a personnel manager I did not know, holding my bulging file, gently asked me not to apply for a job at Rices anymore, and my official relationship with Rices was over.

Nonetheless, as I walked through those departments so familiar in my memory and saw those faces again, some common denominators floated to the surface of my mind. Though many of these people undoubtedly saw me as just another kid in a long parade of high school and college workers who were at times incredible nuisances, those people taught me some significant lessons.

In that society which was Rices during those days of the '70's, there were ways that in which things were done and ways that in which they most certainly were not done. Despite the frustrations of maintaining inventory, rearranging stock, creating work schedules, and keeping up with sales figure to meet/exceed, customers were approached, and help was offered. Courtesy, which began with Mr. Bishop and Mr. Marker, was the standard, and, while fatigue might prevent perfect performance, that was the norm. I remember the careful use of "Mr." and "Mrs." When referring to customers and the kindness shown to the younger workers. Surely there were differences of style and levels of friendship but there was an air of mannerliness.   In that store people were valuable and treated accordingly.

There was also a camaraderie among the workers. Whether in meetings regarding the entire chain or sales competitions, our branch was unified and loyal. While it certainly wasn't Camelot, our store was a place where we watched out for on one another. People laughed across racks and aisles at shared jokes with their colleagues. Employees kept an eye out for special items that someone might like and sounded the alert for good buys. We younger people received advice as the adult employees thought we needed it, and through it all, we stuck together. When Eddie at the delicatessen next door berated a Rices worker for bringing a lunch bag into his restaurant and merely ordering a drink, no one ate there for days. We had an identity because we worked together, and that was a valued commodity.

There were other good lessons for us young people during that time at Rices. I quickly learned how to compute a 20% discount, about marked-down merchandise, and I certainly learned that I had no real talent for the strenuous, demanding job of retail. But despite my ineptitude, I was part of something larger than myself and carried part of the responsibility for the success of that store. What I did mattered, both to the store and to those folks with whom I worked. Because of that, I was careful not to disturb displays or touch any paperwork at the registers as I cleared them early before the store opened. Being careful with mark-up and mark-down sheets helped my friends who managed departments, and so I worked so intensely with those figures that I even dreamed about them. My responsibility to my co-workers was a tangible aspect of my workday, and I didn't want to let them down.

As I remember that time and those men and women from a distance for over twenty years, the most valuable benefit of working at Rices was not my employee discount or a lengthy resume. During those days and nights, I saw adults, adults talking and adults working and even adults arguing. There was no confusion as to who was in charge or responsible, or who could answer a question from a younger employee. They didn't try to force get-togethers with the younger folks, nor did they feign understanding of our jargon or music. They were the people of their time and their interests, and we occupied ours. Now, don't get me wrong; there was no official policy written or was any meeting held to assign roles. They seemed somehow to know that they had a place to fill, just as we did, and there was a sense of rightness and security in those arrangements. We just knew that Mr. Bishop would wear his natty suits and smile and answer questions, and Mr. Marker would joke and call his wife "Dahlin" on the telephone. They showed us, through all of their different styles and personalities, how adults function, and while I never remember a conversation with Chris or Cathy about imitating these people, it all became part of how our world worked.

The importance of such clarity of role and responsibility seems even more urgent in these days of babies in designer diapers and adults with pink hair and multiple piercings. Somehow in our world today there has been abdication of roles, an abandonment of tasks, and every one of every age is all stirred up in a stew. My friend Rene was saying just the other day that kids have it so much harder today than ever before, and she may be right. I can't help but think though that if parents and teachers and adults in general looked and acted like grownups and less like wanna-be bikers and posers, life might not be quite so confusing for all of us. If parents were clear on their responsibilities and the importance of being accountable and in charge, perhaps some of the turmoil might disappear. If young people knew that, despite camaraderie and fun, the adults were present and on duty, it might clarify issues for them. Or maybe at least they'd have somebody to go to for answers. As my fourteen-year-old daughter once remarked, "Mom, you're not my best friend. Your job is to be my mom. Friends I can get anywhere."

So, to my friends of long ago at Rices, I am grateful. They demonstrated patience with my bumbling, they laughed at my jokes, and they corrected my errors. They were grown up, and then and now, that's what young people need. Now it is our turn. I just hope we don't forget how important we might be to someone looking around for an adult.

The Guy Who Always Liked Me

It wasn't too long ago that I found a bit of time with nothing attached to it, and besides, I figured that if I just wanted to sit and think. Well, why not? Donned my favorite flannel pj's, plopped down in my recliner, and proceeded to contemplate.

Out of that pocket of time came the memories of someone whose existence never ceased to make me grin like a Cheshire cat...my friend Bubby. Never did we see each other that we didn't hug tightly, and never once did either of us say, "Why don't you just go home? You're getting on my nerves!" So, here's how it all started.

Maury Wade (my dad) and Jimmy Dozier (his dad) met in a local athletic club; my dad the baseball player, and Bubby's dad was the treasurer. It was the middle 1940's, and this sort of gathering-place was a regular site in Norfolk. And soon Frances and Edna entered the scene, and the four enjoyed lots of laughter and dancing. The story went that, when the ladies needed to visit the restroom, they'd announce to their dates,

"Well, we have to have a meeting," and off they'd go. Apparently it was funnier then.

Into the '50's the two families bought homes in a neighborhood in Virginia Beach without knowing each other's intentions. And that's how we grew up---the Wade kids and the Dozier kids. We even went to the same church just a few blocks away, but in those post-war years that's how life looked. Family, friends, and church. And those particular families even had two girls and a boy each. Life was good.

The only real dissimilarity in our families was that James, Jr. (nicknamed Bubby) had Down's syndrome. Not much was known about that condition, but there were signs that Bubby was unique. He did have the physical characteristics, but what he had even more of was personality. Though he went to live in a residential training school at the strong urging of his doctors, his developing personality was the source of great joy.   As Bub learned the skills he'd need to know in his early years, his far- too-rare visits (as far as we were concerned) were truly holidays as he was always full of laughter, Elvis imitations, continuous hugs, and unadulterated joy.   Back then seeing Bub was like an unending party, and he never called me anything but Nassy Wade!

Once when I was in college, I snagged a seat on a bus of special education majors going to visit the campus of Bubby's facility. My anticipation at seeing my friend was mixed with "Will I even recognize him in such crowds?" As I came slowly down a wide staircase, I looked over a river of people in orange tee shirts wondering, "How in the world am I going to find him?" But the problem never came up, because just as I was scanning all those faces, he saw me at the same moment that I saw him. How could he have recognized me? He didn't know I was coming, but that didn't stop Bubby. We just kept hugging and laughing, both of us so completely delighted to see one another. Those around us stared curiously, wondering who he was and who I was. But Bubby knew and I knew, and that was all we needed!

Some years later Bubby lived in a group home in a traditional neighborhood not very far away from his parents' home. He was quite the leader with his happy personality and high functioning level. Near to the residence was that mecca of wonder...a 7-11. Having memorized not only whose car was whose as well as the work schedule of the entire staff in his home, Bub organized a trip to the convenience store under cloak of darkness with no staff approval or knowledge. When the time came for the escapade, Bubby the mastermind sent them off but remained at the home. The only way the staff knew of the illicit trip was a trash can full of candy wrappers and Coke cans, but Bubby was completely innocent. No demerits for him.

Another encounter many years later brings tears to my eyes as I remember that same burst of love and joy that bathed my heart with these unexpected reunions. I was downtown, wandering through second-hand/antique stores. As I unhurriedly browsed through the panoply of treasures, I heard the bell over the door jingle and casually looked up. There was Bub! In a rare moment of thinking-before-doing, I stood quietly as his group found two long wooden seats and sat down to eat their lunches in heavenly air conditioning. Finally I could wait no longer. Leaning forward, I caught Bub's eye and heard his familiar joy as he exclaimed, "NassyWade!" We hugged each other, and he told me the names of everyone on the benches. Some smiled while others kept right on eating. Bubby and I had a few more words, but then it was time for his crew to move on to their next task. I proudly wore that big goofy grin for quite a while that day.

As we both moved through our adulthoods, we saw each other less frequently. Most of what I knew about his life I heard from his sisters with whom I remained friends. Then he was diagnosed with dementia and became more silent and less sociable, so unlike his chatty personality. When The Call came one day at the end of school, I robotically sat in my car alternately staring at nothing and crying. How in the world could I explain who he was and why I couldn't stop crying?

I went home for the funeral, and Bubby's heart-broken, gentle mother and sisters accepted my offer to read something for them. I had to concentrate on the words they'd handed me, since I couldn't look at all of those faces with whom we'd all grown up. As I got to the end of the items the family asked me to read, I recounted a story about Bubby and his personality and life. Later that week I shared Bubby's story with my special education teacher friend, and afterwards she said, "Well, he's in heaven now, and he won't be like that anymore." I breathed slowly and deliberately before saying, "Well, I'm trusting Bubby will still be Bubby because he was just fine as he was." And he most assuredly was.

Lessons from Chas

My student died today. There was a lot of fog, and a road covered with skid marks, and a dead boy in a truck.

Oh, he wasn't enrolled in one of my classes and had not been for several years. He had graduated from high school, had gotten a job and kept his good reputation, and suddenly he was dead.

So, other than the sorrow I usually feel when a young person dies, why do I feel this wavery empty feeling in my heart? Why do I feel an urgency to call all of my students and make sure that they are all right? Why is it important to try to recollect some specific memories of this young man as a ninth grader?

I suspect these emotions are tied in with the sense of urgency that surrounds most teachers. Unfortunately, too often that sense of urgency has more to do with parts of speech and theorems and dates than with the real issues of life. It's easy to "major in the minors," and in reality, an education is what parents and kids expect to gain from attendance at school. But education is so much more than books and tapes and films and tests. It is, besides all of these strategic things, values and growth that burrow deep into the heart of a child and help to prepare him or her for the journey ahead.

Two questions arise out of musings of this sort. These are not easy questions, but then most folks who are out for easy questions turn to jobs other than teaching. The answers we give to these queries should act as mirrors, in which a teacher can see clearly and accurately who he or she is. Too often we "see through a glass darkly" when what we should be doing is sitting under several glaring light bulbs to examine ourselves.

The first question that slammed into my consciousness after the initial shock was, "Did I say everything, do everything, use every moment to the utmost with this boy?" A quick inventory yielded some achievements, some specific instances of positive influence. I did teach this child some things about English, and he did know that he was valued in Room Seven. We laughed a lot and fussed a little, and beyond that, the memories get vague.

On the other hand, I have no specific memory of a conversation or transaction with this boy that yielded a "Now I understand!" kind of response. There was never, to my recollection, a time of gut-level exchange during which we met as teacher and pupil and came away changed, stretched, matured into new people. If I cannot remember such an interaction with this boy, one of the easy-to-love students, then I must wonder how many other chances have slipped away.

If I am to recoup something from this death, it must be a fresh zeal to redeem the time with every boy and girl God sends to me. I just cannot afford to take a lackadaisical attitude toward a class period, a conversation, or even a glance when it involves the lives and souls of my students. And the simple, painful reason for such passion is both simple and painful -- there are no guarantees when it comes to time.

The second question follows rather squarely on the heels of the first. If the time is fleeting and the kids are constantly on the move, then how can I better use these moments and encounters with these often-enigmatic students? The answer must come from two sources: the Word of God and my response to His call in my life.

The only place to find both wisdom and direction demanded by such a commitment is the Bible. I must immerse myself in Scripture so that the depth and breadth of God's wisdom can invade the very fabric of who I am.

The lamp and light of the Psalms are the only ways to see down those amazingly murky paths. The temporary knowledge of empirical studies, the trendy classroom behavior techniques, and the chutzpah of a brash personality will not provide sufficiently for the myriad of questions and problems that face every teacher. The prayer of every teacher must be that of the Psalmist as he wrote, "Open my eyes that I may behold wondrous truths from Thy law."

But then suppose God answers that prayer, as He is wont to do? What is to be my response, and if it is not what it should be, how can I move from where I am to where I should be? As I walk in obedience and allow Jesus Christ to live His life through me, I must make some practical decisions about my time, my abilities, and my goals. Taking into account my class load, extracurricular activities, and family needs, I must be sure that time -- that quicksilver commodity -- is never wasted.

Lunch times can be spent more profitably than in rehashing old gripes or frying students. Those few minutes between classes are perfect times to touch base with that quiet student who never demands attention. After-school activities provide chances for non-adversarial talks, as well as for sending the message to my students that I care about more than just their performance in my class.

My goal here is not to inject some unnatural gloom-filled element into the time spent with students. My goal is, however, to use every minute as it is provided to touch with God's hand the lives of the students entrusted to me. His wisdom will provide His balance so that His changes can be implemented in their lives.

This particular student stands now in the presence of his Lord. Mistakes made and opportunities lost are of no further effect. But, in my class and in every class sit students on whom those mistakes and lost chances are taking effect daily. Though perfection is unattainable, that fact can never stand as the wall behind which teachers huddle and beyond which students surge. Teachers must tear down the barriers and grasp eagerly every instant of fleeting time. Our students cry out for it. Our God requires it

Letter to the Fourth Singer on the Second Row

Thank you to those anonymous choir members
who keep on showing up week after week with
never a solo in sight and
never their names in the bulletin.

Dear Unknown Choir Member,

Thanks for your faithfulness. You have come on sunny days and in the rain. I've watched as you herded your kids into their respective slots, and frankly, many of fainter heart would have given up and gone home. You've come on crutches and in slings, in grief and in celebration, but come you have. Who in the world ever notices these things, you might have wondered? Well, I did, and even though I never knew your names, I recognized you, service after service. There were times when I was in emotional turmoil, watching my entire world crumble; nothing seemed permanent. It was a great comfort to stumble into church, usually out of a sense of nowhere else to go, and there you'd be. It mattered very much to me, in that time of upheaval, that you were there Sunday after Sunday singing your heart out. Thanks for being a constant for me.

Thanks for all of the work you devoted to your music. It must have been so tempting to rationalize, "Well, I'll just skip this one practice. What difference will it make?" But you made the effort, rearranging your schedule, and filled your seat each practice. How do I know this? During those anxious times I would slip into the back of the sanctuary and listen to you labor over the various pieces. With painstaking repetition you'd repeat notes and tempos and phrasings and didn't give up. Someone else was tending your family and folding your clothes or doing your dishes or listening to the Bible study, all of the things that you could have chosen to do. But you were up there honoring your commitment. Oh, and I noticed that although no one ever called your name during solo time, you listened carefully and smiled encouragingly while someone else stood in the lights to sing. That was a part of your job as a team member, and you held up your end there too. Thanks for all of the vocal elbow grease.

Thank you for your enthusiasm ... your smiles and tears, your intense concentration and deliberate enunciation. You have invested a part of yourself into your music, and it has been a bona fide marvel. Incidentally, the body English that would suddenly appear during some of the more exciting pieces communicated to the congregation your enjoyment of the music, and so we enjoyed it all the more. Your careful attention to cues and directions reminded me that you were there for a purpose, and so was I. So often I felt that the most appropriate ending to your anthem on a Sunday morning would be the benediction, because God had spoken to me through you and your riveting music. Many is the time that I left my cares at His cross to the accompaniment of your songs. Thanks for your energy.

Thank you for your humility. You never seemed to base your participation on public acclaim, which was fortunate for us, since you never did have your moment of glory while I was watching. I'd see you at other church activities, and never once heard you gossip about who was singing what or who flatted when. Your willingness to serve joyfully encouraged me that perhaps there would be a place for me, that God might need quiet service too. As I watched and listened, it became easier for me to be a small part of a big event without hearing that nagging little voice of discouragement that said, "You don't have anything to offer." The dignity and love with which you filled your spot demonstrated the beauty of true humility. Thanks for a willing heart.

Hard times like those are over for me nowadays, and as I live in another community, I see you only on television occasionally. But any time that I turn on the set and watch you sing with your own special pizazz; I think there just might be another one like me out there who is counting on you. Though you don't know who I am, I'll be the one cheering when the Divine Choir Director hands you your crown of faithfulness and says, "Well done, thou good and faithful servant."

Sincerely,
 Third Row, Center Section, End Sea

Nancy Wade Zappulla

Magic at Va. Tech

As I got out of my car, my first thought was to get right back in and drive quickly away. Every one of those grey stone buildings looked like the one next to it, and there were college students everywhere. They were lounging under trees, they were striding purposefully down the sidewalks, they were smashing volleyballs at one another snd I couldn't stand them! I hated them because they all, every last one of them, knew where they were supposed to be and they probably knew that I had no earthly idea where I was supposed to be, and I despised them for it.

It was far too humid to stand in that direct sun while exuding all of that strong emotion, so I began to saunter toward some buildings, glancing oh so casually at my map.

It seemed like a good plan and was going along quite nicely until from behind me I heard a voice. "I'll bet you're just as lost as I am." More than I hate being lost, I hate anyone knowing that I am lost, but years of being nice pasted a cardboard smile on my sweaty face, and I turned to meet Barb. It was somehow more comforting to be part of a lost duo, so she and I together openly consulted our maps, and finally found

Ordered Steps

it - the huge grey stone fortress which would be our home/holding cell for the next two weeks. Barb and I and the nine other teachers of English and/or drama would be studying ways to use theater in our classrooms, and for two weeks we would think and talk and dream of little else. We all started out our adventure with various levels of trepidation and resolve, but start we did. Not much to work with, but Don and Barbara, our dauntless leaders, grabbed our paltry faith and off we hurtled. For two weeks all day and into every night we eleven women, having just met that sultry Sunday afternoon, were stretched beyond our own expectations and, frequently, our own recognition. We zoomed across campus to class, dashed back for meals, and over to the dorm for forgotten supplies or the one-in-a-million chance at the phone. We made letters on the floor with our bodies, we gloried in food we neither shopped for nor prepared, we dissected everything about our profession and students. From the socially comfortable state of pleasing anonymity we were plunged into group showers, lending of washcloths and tote bags, and public partaking of memories of all shades. In between all of these seemingly insignificant events, Barbara and Don demonstrated and explained theatrical techniques and negative space and freedom to create. We ended class with sighs of relief, lots of hugs and promises, and a persona more than a little altered by the experience.

So what? People, especially teacher types, go away to take classes all the time. While we were there at the university, there were all sorts of groups meeting and milling around. What made this particular convergence of eleven so unique? Besides grades, what was the point of it all?

I've spent lots of time thinking about and talking with the ten others, and I'm not sure that there is any one answer as to what made this a success. We were all women, which gave us extra things in common, not to mention all of the extra time for bathroom chat. Nine taught in public school, two in private school. Our ages ranged from 25 to 54, with various and ever-changing marital conditions.

Children were of every age, and teaching assignments fit every arrangement. Some of us trembled at the thought of speaking before adults, while others had to be hauled out of the spotlight. We were early-morning exercisers and ice-cream-every-night lovers. We were the coat of many colors in female form.

Three common threads ran through our multi-everything group, however. We were lovers of language, we were lovers of teaching, and we were ready to take a chance with something indefinable and more than a little frightening. Language began at 5:30 a.m. when the early birds hit the trail. They'd try to whisper, but to the almost-awake ear would come the staccato pieces of last night's unfinished conversation. We'd chat while showering or brushing our teeth, standing in line or zooming across campus. Now this wasn't academic, theoretical mumbo-jumbo being spouted, but that meaty, satisfying back-and-forth of ideas and books and observations. I remember one night that Katherine and I stood leaning on the top bunk of my bed, arms resting on the bare mattress or waving around to make a point. She and I faced one another for almost an hour that night, sharing histories and fears and what-ifs. I went to bed nourished.

Ordered Steps

We talked about being teachers and about our kids and about seating arrangements and administrators and supplies, but over all of that verbal volleyball there came echoing tremendous passion for the sacred art of teaching. New ideas were eagerly snatched and written down in journals, books were analyzed and shared, and I-had-this-kid-who stories never failed to draw an appreciative audience. One of the last nights found five of us in one room, sitting on chairs and floor and bed, laughing and wiping away tears as we shared precious teaching moments. Our salaries never came up that I can remember, nor do I remember talk of getting out or marking time until retirement. What did happen was an unending, portable love story, written by eleven teachers about some of the world's most difficult kids.

All of us were nearly paralyzed by nerves, but just as Nancy was the one to venture up the hall to beam an introduction, we all made a commitment, and having made that decision with as much honesty as we could scrape up, we determined as individuals to milk every experience of those two weeks. For those one or two non-drama folks, the first few days were spent in an endless panic, wondering what everyone else was talking about. Some of us had years of theater experience and wondered if there was an antidote to staleness and routine. There were physical rigors to be faced, for three miles a day up and down those endless stairs was a daunting task. Then, there were those high schoolers with whom we would work. They were real kamikaze actors, stepping on one another to get on stage while some of us teachers were longing for a siesta.

But face it we did, and when the day for departure came,

we faced another kind of shock. Many of us were packed and ready to leave, and yet during the final sharing time, there were unexpected tears. Each woman read her reaction to the experience, but not many eyes met. The downcast or off-in-a-distance expressions reflected each woman's powerful emotions. Bless Don for saving us from an emotional melt-down by unrolling a common roll of toilet paper around the circle. It was good to laugh one final time. The class was over.

We've all kept in touch, and I've been concerned as I've listened to all of the ways that each teacher has integrated all of the new ideas into their classes. While the others have been tearing construction paper and building cubes and handing around dowels and string, I've done none of it. Of course, I teach English, not drama, and we haven't done any plays yet and the cubes will cost me an unattainable $50. So, why did my school waste the tuition money on me? Am I a failure, theatrically speaking?

An explosive "No!" wells up from within what I hope isn't negative space. I learned things from the class on no one's lesson plan, and I grew in directions I'd never had the nerve to glance at before. And by the way, it won't be too long before I'll figure a way to get those cubes built.

I saw myself in a bright white light, and I lived through it. I could take these enormous risks and face success. I, who had never been on a stage, could read some words and see responses on the faces before me. I could expose part of myself to veritable strangers and take those parts home again unscathed. I was stretched to the point of perpetual elasticity, and each time got easier and less painful and, at one point, even approached fun. Words and sentences leapt from me in a confusion of feelings and made sense. Other peoples' words spoke for me and unlocked old fetters and threw open barred doors. Though my exterior undoubtedly grew with all of that ice cream, my interior exploded into new rooms and high clear windows.

For two weeks I was thigh to thigh with women of infinite variety and gifts. Every single person had some great joke to tell or pain to share or technique to pass along, but mostly there was this whole new society being born. Each one found and settled into her role, turning to lift up the stumbling comrade or applaud the first across the line. To sit and listen to snatches of conversations or watch little groups form around a trip downtown or to the bookstore never stopped fascinating me. To watch the dancing class sweatily tapping and black bottoming with a shared grin made it belong to us all. Idiosyncrasies we possessed plenty of, but the three loves we shared gave us somehow the strength to laugh once more and say one more "Okay" regardless.

For my part in the sharing time I began a piece about the magical kingdom of Eothia (named after the sign over the restroom in the hall). It had a great beginning and was moving steadily, and then the voice within me stopped giggling. I didn't want the magic to end, though I was ready to bid farewell to my metal bunkbed. It had to end, I knew that, and I was ready to get on with life and yet, the intoxication of those women and that blip of time was hard to put down. It was a magical kingdom we entered. No, -- we created, and who likes a fairy tale to end? For all of us, it seems that a little of the glitter has found a berth deep within. It may find its way to a student, a piece, or it may just glimmer within our souls. Wherever it lands, there will be newness and excitement and incessant laughter, and most of all, there will be art.

My Daughter Came Home from School

My daughter came home from school the other day with a big grin slathered across her face. Before I could recite the typical "How did your day go?", she began to rattle out an involved story about friends and teachers and lockers. In the midst of her narrative I heard, "And, Mom, choir is so-o-o neat!" Though her story spun on, my mind slipped backwards in time, and suddenly I was in school choir for the first time. Actually, the first thing I remember is having to "try out." I was not exactly sure what that meant, but it did not sound like something Iwould enjoy. I was sure of it when we sixth graders were herded backstage in our auditorium, numbered off in groups of three, and told to sing "Oh Beautiful for Spacious Skies" for this lady playing the piano. I did not know the lady, I was not crazy about the song, and I most certainly did not want to sing in front of my classmates. However, the alternatives, singing a solo or abandoning the choir, were even less appealing, and so when my group's tum came, I stepped up and began to sing. Mid-verse, the lady stopped playing, whirled around on

.....her piano bench, and said, "Who is that?" It was me, and my heart sank. I was as awful as I had always suspected, despite my mother's unceasing encouragement.

I spent the next two years in that lady's school choir, and while I would like to report a substantial improvement in my vocal abilities, honesty prevents me from doing so. This hardy music teacher also directed our church choirs, so she got to listen to me sing on the weekends as well. Figuring that I had nothing to contribute but faithfulness, I would never miss choir rehearsal either at school or at church, and I even learned enough piano to practice my part at home. Each week I would show up, having practiced my part over and over, and each week there would be the same struggle. She'd say, "Listen to your part, Nancy. Just follow what you hear." I would strain and focus and end up singing whatever part the person next to my left sang. After months of this, my director and 'I capitulated to reality, and we always made sure that I was seated to the right of a choir member with pitch. I was loud, but I was not good. I was faithful, and I loved every single thing about music, but I would never sing a solo. I went off to high school and never again tried school choir. The church, being church, had to let me stay, and my director continued her faithful work with me. By then I could read the music; that is to say, I could name the notes, but I couldn't sing them. Sometimes I sang alto, and there was a period of time that I felt called to be a tenor, but through all of the practices and performances, my director kept trying and I kept showing up. So, why is that? Why did I keep showing up, seemingly destined for failure? Why, when I was the one of three children in the family with no musical talent or training, was I the one who took a hymn into my room and sang for God? What made me love this regular exercise in futility? I kept singing and trying, day after day and year after year, because I had a choir director who could, as my mother said, "pull music right out of you." She'd stand in front of us, whether in that silver dress she'd wear at the annual school Christmas program or in her choir robe at church, and she'd smile at us with her high-watt smile and we'd launch off, certain of our success. I suspect that we were always better than we should have been because our director dragged untouched poetry and melody and rhythm from somewhere deep within us. If we made music, and we were always sure we had, it was because our director plunged her hands down deep inside of our souls and pulled up magic.

And now my daughter is in the hands of such a woman. I've watched this lady and felt the same old stirrings within my soul. I've seen the faces of the children in her choir as she stands before them and the magic happens for them, and their faces reflect that wonder. I am thankful for the director that my daughter has, for this woman will give to my child that which I can never give her- music.

Nancy Wade Zappulla

No Longer John Wayne

"Get tough!" That's the advice many people have for teachers today. They argue that "soft" teachers have led to the predicament they're in. If teachers would just stop babying students, stop lowering standards, discontinue listening to excuses and calling them reasons – just cut it out (whatever we are doing) and get a little tougher (what we're not doing). Things would be peachy.

But teachers discover early that no one knows more about this "getting tough" issue than we do, and noting this frightening truth, we begin to scout around. We observe other teachers, mostly those for whom we have either a great deal of respect or none at all, assuming that at the very least we'll see exactly what to do or not to do. We experiment on our students rather timidly at first. If our attempt does not result in a fatality, the next time we try to be a little creative with our efforts. If it blows up in our faces, then we mark that one "Never again!" and pray desperately that no one saw what happened.

Time passes, and we become a little confident of our ability to be tough. We might even see a reputation begin to sprout, and it's the good kind. Kids say things like "You can't mess around in her class!" and brag when they've finally passed. Advice comes quickly to our lips. Soon other crises clamor for attention and fill our minds until, unexpectedly, our rose-colored glasses are snatched away, and we stare into the bare truth of what we have become and flinch at what stares back.

I am a tough teacher. Ask any of my students, especially the upper grade kids, and they'll tell you. I don't accept excuses, and when I say something about classroom demeanor and procedure, that is exactly what I mean.

And I like it that way. I enjoy the me that I have so carefully cultivated, and it is a source of real pride for me. Did you catch that last noun? The word was "pride", and do you remember the quote about something going before a fall? It was pride, and it was mine that recently came crashing down.

On that particular day I had been sarcastically explicit about what I expected regarding deadlines and quality of work to be turned in. No excuses of any kind would be accepted, unless there was blood involved. I gave a stirring speech, and the students were properly cowed. I was aglow with all of that uncompromising authority and even smiled when the bell rang to rescue them. Truly, it was a moment of glory.

Within a few seconds I literally ran into my principal at the classroom door. We extricated ourselves from the collision, and then he demolished me and my pride and my rose-colored spectacles.

"Mrs. Zappulla, I was just coming by to pick up that report – you know, the one that is due today?"

Amidst the tumult of the ensuing psychological crash, I

heard myself ask for clemency and wondered why this moment was lasting so eternally long. He allowed me another day, and I stumbled away down the hall, hearing only the harsh words I had so recently hurled at my students.

That scene played itself over and over and over in my head for several days, and I couldn't dislodge it. I, who was so proud of being so strict, had been placed on the other side of the desk. All of my students' excuses suddenly seemed more plausible. I could visualize their faces in an endless parade as they told me why they needed more time, and I heard my smirky answers. Then, crowding into my view would be the picture of my encounter with my principal, and I'd see myself asking for an extension. It not only humbled me; it began haunting me. I'd see a particular child in the hall, remember his request, and relive my failure all over again. I had to do something, short of changing my career, to interrupt this cycle.

I would like to report that a miraculous intervention has caused me to abandon my quest for quintessential toughness. This, unfortunately, is not the case. What actually took place was no less a miracle, yet it bore no divine trappings, at least, none that you might immediately identify as supernatural. Every time a student came to my desk or stopped me in the hall with a lengthy explanation regarding a derelict assignment, I began to see two images.

Not only did I see that child's face, I also saw mine. Not only did I hear that child's voice, I could also hear mine. Most important, however, the only reply I would then hear would be that of my gracious principal, and then I would find myself extending that same grace of which I had partaken.

Somewhere I had lost my ability to be so merciless.

Oh, my students still have assignments, and they still face deadlines. I have no difficulties speaking sternly to folks caught in some trespass, and I am occasionally angry. But that cloak of intolerance that I had been forced to shed had been, in truth, a heavy burden disguised as pleasure. It had occupied copious amounts of energy to maintain and perpetuate, and all the time I had thought it looked so good on me. But, like my friend the Emperor, I was the only one who thought so. No one else could admire my garment of inflexibility. All that could really be seen was that large measure of effort and time being spent on me. And now that I've thrown that macho mask away, I'm free to concentrate on being an authentic teacher rather than some sort of educational prize fighter.

"And you shall know the truth and the truth shall set you free." CEJ

Nancy Wade Zappulla

Of Caterpillars and William Shakespeare

Even before she exploded into my classroom, I could hear her. "Mrs. Zappulla-a-a-a!" preceded her into the room, and I braced myself for the inevitable yarn. Every day she came in with some Paul Bunyan yarn about passing out or losing her purse or breaking up with the most recent "real true love of my life". A vise grip on the chair before me, tightly clenched jaws, theritual response of "No, you may NOT: these were my regular preparations for the explosion of this particular sophomore into room 206.

I braced myself, and far too quickly here she came. With a gaggle of her current best friends, she dashed in, all of them jabbering at machine-gun rate. For a second, I just watched them -- arms waving and mouths working feverishly. Soon, however, my automatic teacher responses kicked in, and I held up my hands to slow things down.

"Wait, wait, wait! Somebody tell me what's going on" was what I said, but what I was thinking was "QUIET!!" The noise level dropped just a bit, and Toni was pushed forward.

Ordered Steps

"Look, Mrs. Zappulla, look what I brought you! Isn't it cute? It looks just like you!" Propelled by the elbows of her comrades, she revealed my special gift. Latecomers joined the crowd, and within a few moments all 26 sophomores were laughing and making those "Aw-w-w!" sounds so favored by adolescent females --- and all at it!

It was a bright-green caterpillar made of soft rubber. Standing about four inches tall, its oversized glasses were perched on chubby cheeks underneath a bright blue baseball cap. With a face-splitting grin, the little green thing looked over an open book. The overwhelming consensus of the third hour English class was that it was most certainly me.

With a smile more theater than life, I thanked Toni and began my regular quiet-em-down routine. Here I was, my thoughts whirled as I instructed various students to sit down and stop talking, working harder than any teacher ought to have to work during the last weeks of April, and I had to deal with kids like Toni, the one prone to interrupt prayer request time regularly with show-and-tell stories or wails of "I can't find my literature book!" She lived life teetering on the edge of disaster. Teaching "Julius Caesar" was strenuous enough without another day of Toni.

Having gathered the class's attention, I called out, "Okay everybody, turn to page 348 and let's get ready. Today we're going to read this scene in the Shakespearean language. I know, I know, you haven't had time to practice, but let's just give it a try."

Christian schoolteacher or not, I kept my fingers crossed as I surveyed the upshot arms and tried to imagine who would desecrate the Shakespearean language the least. Amidst the waggling arms, Toni's was the most conspicuous. "Me, me. Let me do it. I can, Mrs. Zappulla, I can. Please let me do it! " To stop the flood of words, I smiled thinly and said, "Okay, Toni, you can be Cassius."

The students chosen to participate straggled to the front, bumping into one another and asking, "What page are we on?" With another forced smile I launched the scene, and off they went. The reading was halting and painful to hear, but at least they were reading Shakespeare before their classmates in an upright position. Focusing on this, I was not prepared for Toni's Cassius.

Toni the flighty was reading the scene with clarity and understanding. She was doing all of those things that English teachers obsess about -- reading to the punctuation and taking it slowly and thinking about the words.

Gradually the students also noticed the phenomenon, and the whispering died down. Toni and her Brutus continued their reading, oblivious to the effect they were creating. At the end of the scene the room filled with applause and the familiar shouts of "All right!" as everyone reacted to this unexpectedly proficient Toni.

That scene refused to disappear from my memory, sometimes because other students would ask about the caterpillar on my desk, but more often because of the element of surprise. I had not been surprised that Toni would give me a bright green caterpillar because she thought it looked like me. That fit perfectly my expectations of her.

I was, however, flabbergasted at her ability to read a

very difficult piece of literature with no preparation and had chosen her with great reluctance. Then, as Toni read so beautifully, an awful truth crashed into my consciousness. I, the teacher who glibly lectured younger colleagues on the importance of the student as an individual, almost slammed a door in the face of this student. I expected her to be the crazy one, without allowing her to be the shining one. I was willing to park at the facade without seeking for the soul within.

I could do exactly what I had done that day -- be a respecter of persons, assigning seats of importance at my English banquet table. Not any more! I have placed the bright green caterpillar on my desk to serve both as a rebuke and as a reminder of the wondrous creativity of our God in His creation of sophomore girls. I have also requested new eyes with which to view all of my Toni's from now on.

Tomorrow when I return to my classroom, I promise to peer more carefully past the exterior and beyond the customary behavior. I will more vigorously avoid that sloth of spirit which permits such blindness and will, with equal energy, pursue the hidden treasure that is Toni.

Say, would you like to read some Shakespeare with me?

Nancy Wade Zappulla

Once My Kid, Always My Kid

There are immutable truths in our world today, things that we can depend on never to change, like gravity and Beenie Weenies and computer viruses. In my world, that unfailing something is a student's permanent place on the class list in my heart. Be 12 or be 47, if you were ever my kid, you're still one. It doesn't matter if I see you in class, at the mall, or standing beside your casket, you're still mine.

All that being true, losing a student shatters the heart, whether he appeared in my class yesterday or in 1973. I've lost several of them over the years, and it never gets easier.

Tony had grown up, married, fathered a couple of kids, and then began behaving oddly. One night his former wife (also a student) found him in her house in a closet. There were threats, and phone calls begging friends, "Talk to him; make him stop," and one night God answered that request. Tony drove east on the westbound lane of 1-64, and he died there. It was scary and sad and something of a guilty relief, knowing that he would never hurt himself or anyone else again.

Jessica was one of those witty, quiet girls who could tease with a quick grin and a glint of mischief, and then a "Who, me?" expression. A creative and droll writer, she was too often passed over by folks only interested in glib chatter. She got a part-time job in a library during college, and there she met a shy young man who was able to coax out all that Jessica was. They married, and not a year later, she smiled up at him as he rose first to dress. When he returned from the bathroom, she lay dead. At her funeral this earnest young husband spoke through tears and smiles and downright laughter as he shared his wonderful wife with us. In the receiving line I introduced myself and he replied, "Oh yes, she told me about you. She always loved you." Though my feet walked me away, my heart stood still, moved by the picture of Jess talking about English 11 honors. What an honor she conferred on me that day!

I taught both of the Hunt kids, Marjorie and Jonathan. She was funny and bright and willing, and he was funny and bright and reluctant. Jonathan never did anything in-your-face bad, but he managed to ignore and downright disobey lots of rules. His parents tried everything to help him and discipline him, sending him to a military academy from our Christian school and then to a public high school. He never changed, always happy-go-lucky and eager for a quick hug. He finally graduated, still wandering through life, and on a summer Tuesday he bought a motorcycle. He crashed and died on it that night. At the viewing for more than three hours his parents hugged and comforted and shook hands with church friends and neighbors and high school kids by the truckload. His funeral was the kind you have to clench your teeth to keep from screaming. Until Marjorie graduated and cleaned out her locker, the inside door was covered with pictures of Jonathan, and I used to stop by for a look now and again. She told me once that she knew that he had been doing things he shouldn't, but why could some people who were doing bad be given another chance to repent, and he had to die? I didn't know the answer then, and I don't know it now. I just know that God knows.

There was a class that I got to teach for three years in honors English 8, 10, and 11. Amy was a merry kid, always with a funny story. She loved the arts -- music, art, writing, drama -- and volleyball. She went to college and when I ran into her at the restaurant where she worked, she had to sit down and tell me all about becoming an English teacher. She was so excited, and I was too, because the picture of her in her own classroom was a perfect fit. Her natural ability and enthusiasm would have made her a superior teacher, but one night she hit a phone pole four blocks from home and died. Gazing down at her in the casket, so unlike any posture I'd ever seen this busy kid in, there was my own hurt and an even greater loss that would be the lot of kids who'd never have such a captivating teacher.

And Jason wasted away before our eyes with liver cancer -- the All-State receiver who could run the ball with three defenders hanging on him -- getting thinner and thinner. David died this past summer at 41, but looking down at him in that coffin with his Sponge Bob tie, I knew that the prankster of the class of 1980 hadn't changed one iota. Justin came into the 8th grade for the last semester and spent all of his energy trying to be invisible. He pretty much succeeded, getting attention rarely. He was quiet and did his work, and those things get you a pass in middle school. He drowned this spring, and I felt guilty about how little time I'd spent with him. It probably didn't mean anything to him.

Now I teach incarcerated juveniles, with hundreds of boys and girls moving in and out of my class yearly. Relentlessly they march in and out of our facility, and just as quickly once-empty seats are filled. Despite the seemingly unending supply of kids in trouble, some manage to climb up into our hearts, and when they leave, though they haven't died, we grieve for just a little more time with them. Oh, we might see them on the news or run into them at the mall, but, for the most part, they are changed. Those faces, easily sliding into smiles or creasing with intensity in school, have morphed into guarded masks mumbling some garbled thug speak. Sometimes some of us who work here will bring up the name of one of our alumni, and we'll remember the antics of this one or the ruin of another. But there's no time for that, and once again we begin class, handing out forms and textbooks and going over rules.

So, what's a teacher to do? Some cling to each student with a nearly frantic tenacity, while others maintain a self-preserving distance, repeating robotically, "I'm just waiting until 3:00." Me? I don't know how to articulate some official student policy. I do know two things though, and these principles haven't wavered or disintegrated. Any day is made joyously brighter by seeing a former student, and next to parenting, there is no more important job on this planet than being a teacher.

Nancy Wade Zappulla

Ordinary People, Extraordinary Teachers

These teachers proved that the words
they spoke on Sunday mornings were true.

Climbing into my favorite chair and reaching for the bulging Sunday newspaper, I called a list of instructions down the hall to my child. "Put your Sunday School shoes in the closet and your clothes in the dirty clothes basket. Get shoes on your feet before you go out." As she swished by, she dropped a piece of paper over the top of my newspaper. I wondered what kind of letter was coming from Pastor Eric this week. I was sure it had to do with volunteering in the children's department or giving money or both.

The note, however, was encouraging parents to send notes of appreciation to Sunday School teachers during Teacher Appreciation Week. I closed my eyes and thought of my child's Sunday School teachers. They were not professional educators, but this couple had a powerful, consistent effect on my child.

Ordered Steps

Week in and week out they had spoken, lived, and led their class to God's Word. My daughter regularly told me about something her teacher said about Jesus, who He is, and what He does in the life of a Christian. Many times we discussed the lessons, and I had to scramble to keep up with the truths my child had heard and pondered.

Not only had her teachers presented the Word, they had taught integration -- the way a truth from God's Word becomes part of a life. In the special events planned, the prayer requests remembered, the phone calls made, and the simple moments of shared time with individual children, these teachers proved that the words they spoke on Sunday mornings were true. Out-of-class events have been valuable to my daughter. Trips to the teachers' home for hot dogs and slides of the Holy Land, neighborhood evangelism, cookie-baking projects, and Slurpees have been exciting for a child to anticipate and to remember later. Unexpected phone calls have made my child feel special and loved for her uniqueness. Whenever she says, "Mom, it's my Sunday School teacher," a special smile beams. The details of these conversations and field trips are her treasures.

An important part of this couple's impact on my daughter is that they are a husband and wife team. We are alone, the two of us, and it is vital that she sees a happy marriage in operation. Having a man in her Sunday School class provides that balance and perspective that is strategic. This man doesn't have to do anything spectacular or unusual. He is a man who loves Jesus and his family, and his influence is tremendous. How could I write a note to thank people who do these things? In all probability they see themselves as very ordinary. How could I thank them for filling gaps that nobody else sees or for praying prayers that nobody else prays? These teachers have kept my child focused on Christ when her life was in chaos. Was a thank you enough? Of course not.

But this I can do. I can pray every day for these teachers. I can encourage them in their ministry. Most important, I can reach out to touch someone's life as they have touched my child's. I can learn from them how to make a difference. I can learn from them.

My child's teachers are my teachers too.

Saint Granddaddy

Bending to pick up the picture the cat had knocked off the coffee table for the zillioneth time, I stopped to glance at it once again. This was a favorite snapshot of mine, which is why I had chosen it to be framed and displayed. The house was quiet, and so I sat down on the sofa with the picture still in my hand and examined it once again.

The boy in the picture was about seven years old and posed intentionally. Wearing tennis shoes, dark pants and a dark suit jacket, his white shirt gapped around his neck, which probably meant that it belonged to his big brother. A too-large sports car cap of some tan fabric, a paisley tie hanging below his belt, and an expression which said, "I know something you don't know!" The whole look was topped off by the large book he held open to the camera. This young man was clearly dressed for some specific event and was as equally pleased with the way he looked. As I once again looked at this picture of my nephew

Michael, I also once again remembered the event for which he was so nattily attired. In his school, rather than celebrate Halloween, the emphasis is placed on All Saints'

Day.   The elementary students read about the history and meaning of the holiday, and assorted educational activities take place around that day. The favorite and final event was always the day to dress up. The teachers carefully discussed what a saint is and gave examples of saints to help the students as they began to choose which saint they'd become. Typical examples might be the Apostle Paul or Billy Graham. The students always find this the best part of the All Saints' Day unit, and why not?

My sister-in-law Emma asked Michael which saint he would choose to be, being familiar with the proceedings from Child #1. Expecting Michael to choose one of the more commonly thought-of characters, she was mildly surprised when his answer was, "I want to dress up like Granddaddy." One of the most unflappable moms I know, Emma asked Michael why he had made this choice, but the discussion died. Evidently Michael had made his decision, it was final, and there were other issues more crucial which demanded his attention, such as computer games. Nonetheless, Emma and Michael did assemble the proper accoutrements with Gram's help, and the ensemble was completed. As far as I know, the event proceeded to Michael's satisfaction. He never did see what the big deal was.

But I saw it differently. My reaction was a combination of curiosity, pride, and probably a little envy. What was it in that little guy's mind which connected a holiday honoring saints and a grandfather? Reminded by that picture, I found myself puzzling over this more than once and even asked my sister-in-law what might have identified this dad/granddaddy as a saint. Pointing out that although Michael had seen Granddaddy lead the church services in his church and had probably overheard discussions between his dad and granddad, she couldn't say for sure. It was just something in Michael's mind which identified his grandfather as a saint, and none of us might ever understand the logic of a seven-year-old.

Having done all of that thinking and questioning, I thought about this modern saint who is my father. What a compliment for him, this slowing-down church elder, that his youngest grandchild sees him in this capacity, and I told him so. Laughing with pleasure, Dad assumed his typical Christian/John Wayne stance, acting like this was no big deal. He does that a lot, pushing away obstacles or disappointments or struggles, responding to such situations with a familiar "Well, Lord willing". After his momentary enjoyment, Michael's granddaddy turned to his newspaper or reruns of "Columbo", having things to do just like his grandson did.

So, though the two main characters in this story have moved on, I am still drawn to the picture and the story. Perhaps it is because our world is so lacking of men who are admirable, or maybe it is the sweetness of the compliment. On the other hand, maybe it is just me, sensitive to the idea of legacies. Whatever the attraction, I still find myself telling the story over and over to guests who notice the picture.

Nancy Wade Zappulla

She Was Right After All

Oh no, here comes Mom with another notebook. "Great, Mom. Thanks a lot. Yes, I know. I have had lots of exciting things happen to me. Yeah, yeah." So ran the first 25+ years of my life -- my mother giving me yet another notebook to write in, and me performing every evasive maneuver I could think of. I had no desire to write about my life or anyone else's. Writing, I figured, is what you do if you're too old or incapacitated to do anything else. I was too busy having a life to spend time writing about it.

Then, one sunny September afternoon every teacher's nightmare came true. My mother called with the news that Chas, a former student, had been killed in an automobile crash. He was in his early twenties, and I hadn't taught him since his ninth grade, but that didn't matter. Once my student, always my student had always been my credo. Immediately out of my soul gushed anger and fear and panic. An urge to call the roll -- to check on all of my students -- drove me to call one after another, but there was no real satisfaction. I paced around and around the oak kitchen table, propelled by a mishmash of feelings. I had to do something, but what could I do?

Ordered Steps

From somewhere as unfamiliar to me as the source of those feelings emerged one thing -- I had to write. Despite my mother's encouragement, I'd never attempted to write anything other than those obligatory college English papers. But this, now this was my life and Chas's death, and sitting before that old Royal electric typewriter I felt stiff and overwrought. I also recalled for the first time in a long time what I'd said when I bought that electric typewriter the year of my first job.

"God, " I'd said, "if you'll let me buy this thing, I promise I'll try to write like Mom wants me to." The typewriter went on sale, I bought it, and life went on. No writing took place.

Yet, here I was, fourteen years later, sitting before that machine with a volcano rumbling within. I typed the first sentence: "My student died today." That sentence drew out another sentence about what had happened, and from that time on, one sentence was sewn on to the next one. I typed on and on, and all of my emotions about teaching and my students and life erupted onto the paper.

And then it was finished. I leaned back in the wooden chair, astonished and drained. It had been a catharsis of unexpected power, and yet the teacher in me began to spot word problems and structural imperfections. Four re-writes later the story about my student and the lessons I had learned was as complete as I could make it. "Lessons from Chas" was written, and yet the project seemed unfinished. What was I supposed to do next? I had already done the unthinkable, at least for me. I had written. The next step in my radical adventure seemed predestined. I would try to publish the story.

Since I had taught Chas in a Christian school and the story was written from that perspective, the logical place to send the essay was a magazine for Christian schoolteachers. The emotional adrenalin was still pumping so strongly that I was convinced that this was a fantastic, completely unique scheme. I sent the essay, with no semblance of a query letter or SASE -- I'd never heard of either -- to Christian Home and School, a magazine I'd seen in our school office. It never occurred to me, in my highly charged frame of mind, that the entire Christian publishing world was not holding its collective breath waiting for this essay, and so I was not at all surprised to receive in a week a large white envelope from CH&S. I was surprised, however, to find that my writing was not what the publishers had in mind for their magazine. The letter went on to say, though, that they were enclosing a copy of a magazine which they thought would be more suitable for my essay. Who was I to argue? Immediately I sent the essay to Christian Educators Journal, my expectations altered only slightly.

Within a few weeks I received a letter from CEJ, thanking me for my fine submission and asking permission to buy it for the remarkable sum of $25. Of course, I called my mother to give her a chance to say a well-earned "I told you so!" and then I marked the calendar for the publication date. Imagine, me a published writer!

Since then I've published several other essays, sometimes making more money and sometimes less. Everything that I write still comes from some subterranean desire to speak my piece, and publication always comes afterwards. Have I had rejections?

Ordered Steps

Sure, but not enough to make me put the lid on the typewriter. Besides, since I write primarily for creative ventilation, the purpose of my writing has been accomplished when I turn off the typewriter. I've gotten a computer, incidentally, and no, Mom doesn't give me any more notebooks. She just checks to make sure that I 'm writing.

Nancy Wade Zappulla

Shrines and Student Loans

Yesterday the optometrist commented, "Oh yes, I'm just going for a quick master's, you know. No big deal."

Well, maybe his isn't, but my newly-framed diploma is not only special, it teeters dangerously close to holiness. Nothing special indeed. I suppose lots of people go back to college nowadays.

The staff at those venerable institutions have labeled us adult students, and since we are often older than our professors, we're okay with that. Most of us don't have time to get drunk and wear lingerie on our heads, so yes, we are adults. We are supporting families and borrowing huge sums of money (which means we will be supporting our government for years to come), while we scribble undecipherable notes and stare down computers and try to ignore being spoken to as "Ma'am" by our classmates. Yessiree, if any of that makes us adult students, I'm in the club.

So, I chose to turn 40 on the campus of my long-ago undergraduate high-jinks, Radford University. I took my nine-year-old daughter, signed a zillion documents regarding my past, current, and future financial life and began graduate school.

Ordered Steps

During that year my daughter had her first job, I began wearing reading glasses, and we moved three times. Throughout these luminous events were laced pages of readings, the schizophrenia of living both on campus and in the community, and hands aching from the unfamiliar exertion of taking notes. Because of the patience of the library staff, a concerted effort on the part of the education faculty to be rid of the pre-menopausal lady in the pink sweatshirt, and the fervent prayer of Alice while I took my orals, I graduated. It was over, I had a job, and I could add that

M.S. after my name.

We settled into our new city and our new life, and graduate school dropped away into memories. Every once in a while, we called special friends, the student loans bills began, and one day the diploma came. No heralds, no spotlights, just a large cardboard flat stuck in the door. I was delirious with pride and displayed it constantly. And life went on, and the white cardboard flat was stored on top of the shelf for safety. I checked the price on framing it one day and replaced the diploma quickly on the shelf. Maybe when the income tax refund comes in, I thought.

And the income tax refund came in, and the bills gobbled up all the money. And two years passed. Finally, this year the edge of the flat hung over the shelf just a bit when I was dusting, and I pledged to put the money aside somehow. And the check came, and I did. And today my master's degree is hanging on a rather bumpy white bedroom wall just above a lopsided dresser lamp. It looks a little out of balance perhaps, but I planned it that way.

You see, just to the right of the big impressive diploma is a snapshot, carefully matted to match the formal document. In the picture Claire and I stand stuck together in a crowd on that muggy May Saturday. My cap is askew, and the big sunglasses are overwhelmingly un-intellectual, but the focal point is us. Amidst the chaos the two of us, kid and mom, made it. So, the framed diploma is a tribute to our small but tenacious family, the two Zappulla women.

There is a big white space above that snapshot, and depending on the glint of the light on the glass, I see different faces reflected there. There were, during our time at Radford, people who hoisted our sagging spirits, gave us things to laugh about, and offered solutions to what seemed to us like insurmountable obstacles. There were deans and directors who pointed us in the right direction and cried along with us when we took a wrong turn. Housekeepers and professors shared sage advice and taught us confidence. Secretaries all over the campus answered endless questions, kept an eye on the younger member of the family while Mom was in class, and prayed during exams. So, although only two signatures make this diploma official in the eyes of the State Department of Education, there are many more names which made it real.

Overall of these human efforts, herculean though they were, arched the loving arms of the Father God, who moved in people and situations to make this diploma much more than the impossible dream it had always been. Many times, as I walked across campus, the love of a God who would allow me to spend another year at this most beloved place snatched my breath away. I wondered if others saw the huge red gift ribbon wrapped around that campus. That's what it was, you know. Spending that time at RU was a divinely wrapped present for me, and that diploma on the wall reminds me of His remarkable love for me with every glance.

Shrines are pretty scarce in the lives of Americans these days. For one thing, we don't have the time to stop and regard anything as holy, and then there is that entrenched cynicism. Too many special places and people have been debunked before our eyes, and we just can't believe in much of anything anymore. And don't forget, the word these days is "proactive": we must be the ones to make things happen. Well, that diploma hanging on the wall is the closest thing to a shrine you'll see in my house. It reminds me of a God who loved me enough not only to send His Son, but to send me, and in the sending, proved how even student loans are love gifts.

Nancy Wade Zappulla

They're Not Playing My Song

Spring is the time for try-outs. Plays, sports, musicals—all over schools there are posters and announcements about the assorted teams and events, and everywhere there are nervous young people, clutching scripts and gloves and clubs.

Yesterday the aspiring softball player in my house invested in a new pair of cleats, and nutrition has become an important topic of discussion. She, like the others, wants to make it through try-outs.

All of this angst has reminded me of the time I tried out for something. Not possessed of any great athletic talent, I never went through the multi-stage agony of sports try-outs, but one time I did audition for a choral group. Looking back, I am sure that I was insured a spot in this chorus because everyone could take the class, but I didn't know that then.

It was the fall of my seventh grade, and there was a new music teacher. Each aspect of this situation was thoroughly dissected at the lunch table, on the bus, and on the playground. What would it be like, the audition? What would you have to do to make the group? Only those students already committed to the band program were oblivious to the tension which we fed with our unending conversations.

The day arrived too quickly, and the teachers sent all of the students from each of the three seventh grade classes to the cafetorium, that favorite architectural wonder of the '60's. A piano sat far back amid the curtains on the stage, and while no one eating lunch could actually see us, we felt exposed. The process was explained quite casually by the new teacher. We were to come up in groups of five, stand behind her as she played the piano, and sing "My Country 'tis of Thee" in our best voices. We looked at one another out of the corners of our eyes and backed slowly away so as not to be chosen first.

I don't remember where in the sequence of singers my group fell. Since each group was dismissed after singing, the groups waiting to sing had a smaller and smaller audience as time went on. Our group was finally called, and we assembled ourselves in the proscribed fashion. The familiarity of growing up together drained away, and we felt like strangers clustered together facing that unfamiliar back. As she had done several times before, the director began playing, and we all launched forth into what we were sure was our funeral dirge.

"Who was that?" she exploded, shocking us into silence. In no other group had she stopped playing nor had she made any editorial comments before, but with my group, there was this agonizing interruption. She repeated the question again, only this time she looked directly at me. I prayed for death for one of us, I didn't much care which, and then it was over.

My memory is merciful, and I don't remember any other part of that day. I did make that choir, and I did come to love that lady who terrified me so. She loved me too, I think, perhaps out of desperation. I was the one student in her choir who could never hear the alto part nor could I sing it once she played and sang it for me. Perhaps it was because I liked singing so much or maybe it was because she enjoyed a challenge, but whatever it was, we were great friends for years. I never told her how devastating her unthinking reaction had been to me. Maybe I didn't want her to remember how badly I really sang. On the other hand, it occurs to me that having lived through such a genuine trauma at thirteen was part of building some crucial part of my character. One thing is for sure, however, I don't sing on stage anymore!

To Be the Parent of an Abused Child

To be the parent of an abused child is to tread water in an ocean of anger, fear, and fatigue with no shore in sight. These emotions may vary in frequency and intensity, but there is rarely a moment when a parent does not wrestle with these three gut-wrenching feelings.

The anger that accompanies the shattering disclosure of child abuse is frequently unfocused and often showered on unsuspecting passersby. Although the rage is aimed specifically at the perpetrator, it still oozes into daily activities as disconnected as cooking, working, driving, and on and on. The secondary focus of this anger is difficult to accept, because this non-abusing parent faces an anger against him- or herself. "If I'd only" runs through the mind of the mother or father like a broken record, and that sort of self-damning dialogue perpetuates the fury at oneself for allowing this abuse to occur. That this attitude is frequently illogical lessens its impact no less. There is also, unbelievably and yet honestly, an anger at the child. Although most parents who believe the child's story would argue that of course they feel no anger toward their child, these same parents achingly reveal a small piece of enmity toward the child. Taken all together, these sources of anger generate a climate of constant tension for the parent, as he or she struggles to live as a civilized human being without projecting all of this fury onto the rest of the world.

The fear in which these parents live comes from the loss of control resulting from the knowledge that, despite their best parenting skills, their child has been violated. This message destroys the confidence of the strongest of parents and is usually followed by a frantic scrutiny of every person and situation in their child's life, past and present. To discover that the best protection has failed is to open the terrifying possibility of future harm from which the child may once again be unprotected. In other words, the fear is about past events, the current crisis, and the yawning future, full of terrors yet undefined. Is it any wonder that the parent is apt to bounce from one extreme of child surveillance to another?

The fatigue that envelops this parent is bi-level, affecting both physical and emotional functions of life. Because of the interaction between body and spirit, this parent cannot eat and sleep in a normal fashion. The unusual exertions of being involved with therapists, detectives, doctors, and attorneys bring more stress to this parent who, in most cases, has no experience dealing with these systems that have burst unwelcomed into his or her life.

A more intense supervision of the child, new acting-out behaviors from the child, the need to relocate -- these are but a few of the factors that sap the physical and emotional strength of a parent and sustain the cycle of fatigue. For the parent of the abused child, there is no such thing as a good night's sleep or a day off. If these are the three overriding emotions that impinge so heavily on the parent of an abused child, what help can

the concerned school counselor offer? The most strategic position is one of concern, awareness, and availability. To say to a parent, "I know how you feel," is an insulting lie, unless the counselor has been abused, but to say, "What are some things I can do to help you?" gives the parent a chance to ask for extra time for assignments, assistance in increased supervision, or even a listening ear.

To be aware means that the counselor knows state and local laws, knows the child and his or her schedule well enough to provide practical help, and knows some community resources to suggest. Being available does not mean allowing the parent or child to monopolize the counselor's time, but it does mean providing sufficient time for the genuinely critical issues. Perhaps the counselor and child can arrange a secret signal so that the counselor will know when he or she is truly needed by the child. Availability means providing necessary documentation, without delay, for legal matters without complaining or excessive bureaucratic interrogation. The unfortunate fact is that no school counselor can solve this tragedy. The good news for the compassionate counselor is that, amidst a family's life-altering crisis, an informed, sensitive, available school counselor can ease the way and provide the consistent support that can give both parent and child an opportunity to survive.

Nancy Wade Zappulla

To the Mighty Class of 1989

Does it seem strange to you that we are together again, and you're not struggling to write down my every word and I'm not holding forth on English poetry? It seems strange to me, and I'm not at all sure that I like it. Our former arrangement seemed so pleasant – me, prattling on forever and you taking reams of notes.

And yet, here we are, smack dab in the middle of graduation night, but for some reason I cannot keep my mind here. It keeps wandering over the past 180 days, stopping only to chuckle or swallow a tear. Do you remember my explaining the meaning of the word ambivalent? It means feeling or thinking two different ways about one idea. And ambivalence is my state now

-- glad to see you achieve your goal of graduation, and yet somehow wistful to think that those amazing days of your senior year are over.

One thing I will always remember about your senior class is the never-ending sense of humor which accompanied your entrance into my room daily. You made me laugh when I was determined to be proper, and I need to say here and now that I needed to unbend a little. Thanks for the starch removal.

Yours has been a class remarkably devoid of nitpicking and backbiting. While you have doubtless had disagreements, you have been the consistent good friends to one another that the rest of us need to be. I've heard you defend one another when it would have been easier to be invisible. You have seen good qualities in people who aren't your best friends, and you have shared that perspective. I hope we remember to do that as well as you have.

Class of '89, you have been passionately fair and asked that from the rest of us. You have most politely questioned procedures and in doing that have made at least this teacher more concerned about justice. Never once have I heard a complaint from you without also seeing a willingness to help right the wrong. It is awfully easy to complain and just as hard to make changes, but you have helped to remind all of us about equality and fair play. We've needed that.

Have you ever heard the saying about not leading with your heart? I didn't think so, because you twenty have shone day-in and day-out compassion and mercy. You've listened to stories long since gone stale; you've allowed elementary kids not only to buy you, but also to hang all over your limbs; the ways that you have spoken up to help another student or teacher have acted as mileposts for the rest of us travelers. Each time one of us comes this way again, we'll be reminded to show the hearts you have bared to us.

I'd like to give you just one last vocabulary word, and you will be tested on this. The word is diligent and can be defined as " ... steady and earnest application and effort." I can promise you an A+ on this vocabulary test, because all of you have exhibited this quality. You have unstintingly taken notes, borrowed someone else's notes to crosscheck your own, and then read my book, just to make sure. Though some of you have English teachers hiding in you (and you know who you are!), you have been on your studies, as they say in the South, like a duck on a June bug. Because you've been so intense, I've been a better teacher.

Of you will be remembered singing in the halls, the great efforts on field and court, driving a special car, phone calls over term papers, mugs, late-night swims, lengthy discussions, and soul-honest prayer. With you in our halls, life has been spicy, unpredictable, and most joyous. Will we miss you? Absolutely not. You have so indelibly imprinted our school with your uniqueness that I expect for years to come folks will catch a glimpse of someone they're sure is you. We're thankful for you, and also for those folks who did without to send you here. Without them, you wouldn't be the young people whom we come here to honor.

Here are my final thoughts from our friend Mr.

Stewart. Listen to the words.

May the good lord be with you, Down every road you roam,

And may sunshine and happiness Surround you when you're far from home.

May you grow to be proud, dignified, and true. And do unto others as you'd have done to you. Be courageous and be brave

And in my heart you'll always stay Forever young.

Ordered Steps

And when you finally fly away
I'll be hoping that I served you well. For all the wisdom
of a lifetime
No one can ever tell.
But whatever road you choose, I'm right behind you, win
or lose. Forever young.

Love, Emily Dickinson Zappulla

Nancy Wade Zappulla

What the World Needs Now Is Logic, Sweet Logic

With what amazement did I read today that, according to The Washington Post, White House officials are stunned to discover that Dick Morris is only "...out for himself." The article, entitled "White House has had it with Morris," recounts the shock of many officials who have been appalled by the egotism and self-absorption of Mr. Morris. Is it just me, or did this fact seem obvious? If a married man has a lengthy extramarital relationship and other encounters which are more of the short- term variety, could he not be described as consumed by himself? He certainly was not consumed by his marriage and family. Would someone of this ilk be considered to be self-centered only in some matters and not in others? Or, is it illogical to think that even though Morris did not put his family obligations first, he would put his loyalties to the White House ahead of his own interests? Boston Globe columnist Ellen Goodman laments the loss of civility in a recent column ("Anonymous flame throwers scar nation"), citing the absence of community as the raison d'etre for the mannerlessness of some citizens. She cites several examples of vulgar comments on the Internet masked by code names, obscene hand salutes from faceless drivers whizzing by, and the unnecessarily swallowed bitter pill of chance, the debilitating idea that some random cosmic event produced me and thee. Or even worse, how many folks have come along with their ears crammed full of the "man is just another animal" insult? These two concepts, followed to their logical ends produce the inevitable irresponsible, self-centered louts who foist their insults upon us all.

Another illogical conclusion has been bandied about by the press recently. The Character Issue, as it has been named, is of great concern in this election year, and the scenario goes something like this: Person A, someone of fame, has been found with a moral skeleton in his/her closet. Some illegal, yea, immoral behavior dots the landscape of that person's past, but not to worry. The party/company/university with which he/she is currently associated assures the audience that those old glitches aren't really relevant. I mean, after all, if the person can perform his/her current task adequately, who cares? So, what if Swell Person A broke some laws, inhaled, committed adultery, lied, or made some other "mistakes"? After all, that was then, and this is now, right? Just sweep it under the rug, move along, and life will be rosy. But here comes logic, which reminds us that people's behaviors are generally consistent (apart from divine intervention), and so the people who break laws, avoid responsibilities, and play fast-and-loose with decent behavior will replicate that same old pattern. Of course, theoretically people can choose the realities upon which they base their priorities. But we told them, "If it feels good, do it" and they have taken us at our words. We said, "You deserve a break today," and they've taken it. "We do it all for you" has convinced them that the world has, in fact, been created and maintained for their benefit, and they have acted accordingly. Plainly put, with no strongly articulated and preserved parameters and the autonomy we thought would set them free (which has only convinced them we don't care) piled on top of our hormonally-driven society, the young people who are impregnating one another, shooting one another, and then singing about it are the logical products of the world views of parents who are making so much noise lamenting possible corporate downsizing that they are, as always, oblivious. You see, children, logic must prevail.

And yes, there are exceptions to every situation, and the papers report far too few of those rare stories. Folks who should never make it do, and we rejoice at those fly-in-the-face accounts. Nonetheless, these few examples represent a plethora of opportunities to save the day, or at least the situation, if some basic logic were to be consistently applied. Some things maybe even logic won't fix, but at least we could stop being sucker- punched so often. Just remember, start with the beginning, go step by step, and discard anything more hip than "Do unto others as you would have them do unto you." That's a pretty good place to start.

When Father's Day Presents a Problem

Dear Phyllis,

Well, school has ended, and I know that you worry about what to do with the kids, especially at this middle-school age. They don't want a babysitter, but you sure can't leave them home alone. Another of the joys of single parenting! Speaking of which, if you're like I am, you're probably trying to figure out how to handle Father's Day. For a couple of years, Claire and I went out to lunch, and using a suggestion I'd read somewhere, I tried to initiate discussions about good fathers we know. It was a nice theory, but we both felt pretty phony about it. I don't know what we'll do this year. On this particular Sunday in June, we don't fit in.

The car is making a strange new noise, so I guess I'll have to ask the guy downstairs for some help. Having financial struggles is no picnic, but that doesn't bother me as much as this business of always needing help. There are lots of repairs I can do, and I get out my trusty red toolbox and do them. But some things are beyond me. Do you ever get the feeling that single motherhood is as much about begging as anything else?

I was thinking about that just the other night. I was sitting on the porch after supper with my feet propped up, and instead of fantasizing about winning ten million dollars, I imagined a way to get off this treadmill of missing out and having to ask favors. Here's what I dreamed:

First of all, I'd place each single mom and dad in a partnership with an intact family. The husband and wife would act as prayer partners and sounding boards for the single parent. Wouldn't it be great to get another opinion and to have a listening ear when things get crazy? And this partnership could be reciprocal, so the single parent would have chances to help the intact family as well. I like to have opportunities to minister too. I'd have adult Sunday school classes organized by something other than marital status. I'd love the chance to study and pray and discuss with married people, to enjoy the exchange of ideas among men and women in a Christian setting.

I'd have a list of church members and their skills and talents, people -- including single parents -- who can baby-sit, cook, sew, work on cars, or fix leaky faucets could be included on a master list. Church members who need help could call people on the list. Payment could be in the form of bartered trades. This would be great for all of us with limited income. I'd be glad to trade some tutoring or baked goods for a diagnosis of my car's problems from someone I trust. Everyone could benefit from this.

And what about those annual single-parent father/son or mother/daughter banquets, or sweetheart banquets? Now, you and I agree that these are positive events. I'm wondering, though, if children without one parent or a spouseless adult couldn't fit in somehow. What if the parent/child-oriented events were changed so a child could draw the name of an adult who might otherwise stay at home? Children could make the acquaintance of some of the adults in the church, and vice versa. Wouldn't that minister to a lot of lonely people?

As for a sweetheart banquet, could we find some way to display and honor love that would include all who'd like to participate? Why not have a Secret Pal Banquet after a week of special surprises? We could use that familiar tradition to teach our children -- and each other -- what godly love is all about.

Back to the Father's Day problem. I certainly don't want the church to stop honoring fathers. But how do our children feel when the Sunday school crafts are for dads, and they can't get involved. What if the kids of single moms could be adopted for that day (by a family they know, of course), and the kids could spend Father's Day in an intact family while the single mom could have some personal time?

Does this sound too wild, too impractical? I love my church. And I know my fellow church members would be glad to help me if they knew how difficult things can be as a single parent. I think I'm going to open up and tell them. What do you think?

Love to you and the kids.

Sincerely, Nancy

Nancy Wade Zappulla

When I Grow Up, I Want To Be Just Like...Who?

"Example is not the main thing in influencing others, it's the only thing," said Albert Schweitzer, and so say I. The majority of young people who populate our juvenile detention facilities are the products of a variety of influences. We who work with incarcerated juveniles can't control our students' pasts, but we are responsible for life while they're in our care. And yes, while safety and security preclude certain niceties of interaction with them, we hold in our hands the gift of being positive influences during a critical juncture in their lives.

The truest truth is that we are all -- line staff, teachers, administrators, medical folks -- going to have some measure of influence on these juveniles. We are part of their environment as we work, and they are eternally listening to us and watching us. What sort of model we are to them -- well, that's pretty much up to us. Here are just a few of the ways we influence the juveniles with whom we work:

1. What sorts of words do we use when we talk to them? Are our conversations full of scathing comments, sarcastic

"jokes", or doublespeak? Saying "I don't have time to answer such ridiculous questions," or "What makes you actually think I care?" reinforces the use of language as a weapon. Too often such language is excused as exercising control when it really is, is a kind of bullying or macho exhibitionism. Kids whose ears bear the bruises of verbal assaults shouldn't have to endure them from us whose directives are protection and education.

Coupled with the words we choose is our tone of voice. Wrapping our conversations in scorn, disrespect, and belligerence screams our disdain for our kids and transmits that same negative opinion they've heard before. We need to check ourselves before we blurt out the first thing that springs to mind. Perhaps the excuse is, "I was just kidding," but interestingly, the root meaning of sarcasm is flesh tearing. Do we really want to injure young people that way?

Our facial expressions and body language often send messages even more potent than our words. Saying all of the correct words with a civil tone is obliterated by a scowling face or belligerent stance. We can't forget that the world has not been a pleasant, predictable place for our young people, and they see antagonism where it might not be intended. It is up to us, the adults, to match our words with our faces, and no, we don't always feel like it. Nonetheless, we can't shrug it off, rationalizing, "They'll get over it." Maybe yes, maybe no.

No big news here, but stress is a constant in the world of corrections. We never know from moment to moment what could happen next. Schedules aren't merely flexible, they're liquid. People's lives change at the crack of a gavel. We who work in juvenile detention must how people handle stress with control and even maturity. How do we expect them to handle stress when we burst into flames when things don't go as planned? How we work through changes and problems provides powerful opportunities to talk about and demonstrate our methods of handling stress. Remember, even sullen eyes still see.

How do we relate to our colleagues? Do we roll our eyes and mutter when we see them coming and then laugh it up with them when they arrive? Do we open up our can of smarty-pants in front of the students, demonstrating yet again the hypocrisy of "Don't do what I do, do what I say!"? We must model ways to accept correction and even criticism with dignity. These young people have watched adults do and say a lot of things, but rarely have they witnessed good manners in stressful situations. Let your kids see how a lady or a gentleman behaves.

Perhaps the most powerful example we can offer is one of consistency, of being a person whose words and actions match. Attached to this unswerving commitment to being constant day in and day out must be the willingness to be...dare I say it?...wrong. Sometimes we make mistakes, and we need to apologize. If I offend a student in front of the class, I need to apologize in front of the class. As a veteran of many mistakes and apologies, let me assure you that your authority can remain intact after such a bold move. The kids don't forget, you know, and when you say in front of the group, "Hey, yesterday when I called Devin a slob, I was wrong. I apologize, Devin." Then life goes on, and you're done -- until the next time. When you are predictable with your actions and words, you have modeled something quite novel to your kids...what it means to be a person of integrity.

Ordered Steps

Surely few of us wake up, climb out of bed, and get ready to go to work scheming to be a negative influence on the kids. But simply not planning to be a bad role model isn't enough; we must intend to be a good model with constructive words and actions. What we must be is a role model worthy of imitating, an

adult who demonstrates life lessons these young people may never have seen before.

Besides, you are an influence, whether you want to be or not. We adults have a certain amount of power here in a juvenile detention facility, be it from size or control or a set of keys. "Hey, I'm just here to do my shift" falls far short of reality and is nothing less than an abdication of responsibility. Incredibly susceptible to our influences, these young people are separated from familiar people and pressures. We cannot forget that they are captive audiences floundering in a sea of anger, fear, and sadness. We cannot squander this fleeting opportunity to offer them some other choices in behavior and attitude. When we let this chance pass us by, we take our places in the squadrons of those who could have made a difference but didn't.

Nancy Wade Zappulla

When Reading Became Cool...Accidentally

Recently I read a study, and, within the discussion section of this lengthy article, two sentences stood out like neon. Checking out books from the library does not improve reading skills. One must actually read the book in order to experience reading improvement. Really!

As the English teacher and librarian in a school program in a short-term juvenile detention center, I am a living witness to the veracity of those seemingly obvious statements. Six years ago, there were books in bookcases in the classrooms and in the dayrooms of each of the four living pods. I'd hazard a guess that the vast majority of those young people could read those books. However, a student reading was rarely spotted.

You see, an overwhelming majority of the students were strangers to the idea of reading for enjoyment and saw no reason to change. How often did I hear a student respond to my question, "Would you like me to get a book for you?" with, "I ain't read no book"? Factor in the requisite peer influence, and you can understand why nobody was reading around here.

Ordered Steps

This would be the time that I disclose the magical formula which turned our sullen, disinterested students into devourers of the written word, if there were one. Things changed, for sure, but completely by accident... or providence. Today we have a tiny little space with about 3,500 books, and students who whine petulantly, "Ain't you got no new book, Mrs. Zappulla?" Today reading, tomorrow grammar.

So, in case you'd like to give it a whirl, here's what we discovered:

<u>The first step in creating an environment of readers is to find out what they're interested in</u>. Early on, Robert said, "I want to read about how to do stuff," and further questioning led to buying books on building, landscaping, and such. Ask about the books you might have around the classroom or other places in the building. Bring books from home; they may not be interested, but you'll begin to get a picture of what kinds of books might appeal to them. And when they tell you what they want, write it down. That lets them see that you're taking them seriously, not to mention acting as a memory prod. If they mention unfamiliar authors or books, write down as much information as you can elicit. Personal suggestion: always wear clothing with pockets and carry sufficient paper to jot down the information about the books. Also, remove these papers before you do laundry.

Make it your mission to <u>get the books as quickly as possible.</u> If you can't find the book, update the student promptly. If you don't produce either book or update, they will be relentless in reminding you. Or even worse, they'll write you off as yet another one of many who don't mean what they say.

And besides, this persistence in getting the book they want is a sign that your idea is catching on, so don't squelch it. Encourage it.

Let them see you reading. Okay, maybe that's a fantasy-- the idea of reading in front of your students, but you could talk about what you're reading in your free time. The whole idea is to show them that reading is important to you and not just because you're a teacher. And by the way, enlist the support of your colleagues in talking about books. This may be startling to your students, seeing folks read voluntarily, but forge on.

Regularly bring books to class and do a version of Show and Tell. If you choose books with engaging titles and covers, the students will be interested. You can say, "You know, I haven't gotten a chance to read this. Do you think you could check this out and then get back to me about it?" This could require that you allot time in class for reading for... well, let me be honest... pleasure, but that is part of education, right? Remember the quote about actually reading the books? The more my cherubs read, the more they want to read, because their reading skills are growing.

Have reading contests. and have them often. Let the folks in one class read in competition with another class or chart the numbers of pages one group reads versus another. Last fall for ten days (including weekends) my 28 students read 28,888 pages in a contest between pods! What a great thing for folks to be bragging about... pages read, rather than less-than-legal activities! And in case you're thinking "I don't have time for this sort of thing," who does? And yes, you do have to become a cheerleader of sorts, but what better reason to shake a pompom than students learning to love reading?

Buy and freely _give away -- bookmarks_. Because I stress that our books are important, and corners turned down are an offense against all things sacred. Finding cool bookmarks has become my quest. Currently, exotic cars and custom motorcycles top the list of favorites though some gravitate more toward marine mammals. Fortunately, there are scads of bookmarks which can be ordered at reasonable prices; just get a variety. Ask regularly, "Who needs a bookmark?" and before long they'll ask for themselves. I suspect the requests for bookmarks have something to do with feeling valued and enjoying a bit of personal attention but isn't that part of working with kids?

A crucial support to the love of reading in our program has come from the detention staff. Though their primary function revolves around safety and security, the influence they wield is mighty. Therefore, when a staff person weighs in on the positive side of reading, the impact is mighty and immediate. Our staff does this in many ways, from talking one-on-one with students about books they've both read, to participating passionately in discussions, to saying, "Hey, let me look at that book," when I'm passing books around to stimulate interest. More than once a staff has pointed out a student with a suggestion for a book or politely reminded me that I was supposed to get this book for that student. Our staff is much more than muscle, that's for sure!

Another vital component of our reading phenomenon is the _formal and informal support of the facility administration_. Our administrators have stood side-by-side with the education faculty in providing books, incentives, and those personal moments of recognition that our kids crave. The space and décor of our library was created by our administration team, as well as a fruitful relationship with our local public library. This partnership has produced regular book donations to our library and brand-new books for our students.

<u>Tell everyone you know inside and outside of your school the amazing stories of your students' love of books</u> ...and then share those stories with them. Many people have pictures in their heads about "those kids" we teach, and often these images are highly inaccurate. Sharing stories reminds me what an incredible reading world I inhabit, and I need those reminders. Others who hear the stories go away with their perceptions altered, and sometimes they donate books. Here's how I get to tell those stories. Whenever I get a chance to slip in words like "school" or "my students", I do, and the regular response is, "Oh, where do you teach?" Maybe the responder is just being polite, but when I answer, "I teach at the juvenile detention centers," they're hooked. Usually they mutter something about terror or how they could never work with such kids, and I'm set to go. There's a certain kind of triumph in watching a skeptical expression morph into one of amazement, and besides, the truth will set you and me and everyone else free, right? And when I report these conversations to my kids, you should be a fly on the wall to see their reactions. Sharing these anecdotes with the kids brings such smiles, you can't imagine.

Now you know what happened in our juvenile detention facility, and you can adapt some of these ideas in yours. There are no guarantees attached to these suggestions and accounts; okay, maybe there is one. I guarantee that the results, whatever they may be, will be well worth your efforts and the reverberations will go on forever.

Nancy Wade Zappulla

World Views and a Shoe

The inside of my head resembles far too closely a large, dust-filled warehouse with shards of cobwebs dangling from unreachable beams. Windows smeared and resistant to light and a floor littered with boxes in no apparent order add to the abandoned atmosphere. Unexpectedly, a small dust explosion grows over in the corner, and a small, forgettable man scurries from box to box. Shaking each box vigorously, he mutters, "Nope, nothing in there," and scurries to another where he repeats his litany.

That's the process that grinds away each time that I find a piece of an idea and look for ways to develop it. Some days the little man that is my brain gives up after an afternoon of box- shaking, his back aching and his glasses smeared. Other times he is rewarded with a rattle of an idea, and away he carries it. So, for days there has been the discouraging box searching and the unfortunate silence in response. No more than a title to use as a spark is certainly a beginning less than auspicious, especially when the "want-to" is so commanding, so what then -- or now, as the case may be?

So, perhaps the story is not in the solution but in the

process. Mrs. Wilkerson would have us believe that the method is crucial; that we must follow step-by-step processes to achieve our goal. So, what have been our steps?

"Seventeen leaders and not a follower in the bunch" was my first introduction to you as eighth graders. Mrs. Gillette lauded your creativity and encouraged me to harness it, or at least to corral it every once in a while. Despite the Michelles and their books, Terry and his giggles, Tina and her interminable prayers, and the visitation of the others from Mrs. Smith's room, we created. In committees with raised voices over who was going to do what and how and when and with whom, we designed the Lots of Ways to Get More A's book and game, though we never did get that dice to actually roll (oh no, a split infinitive!) . That door between the two rooms constantly yielded Andre's face or Amy's smile, and there's no point in mentioning where Jack was during all of this. So, we spent the year complaining about the spelling books ("Mrs. Zappulla, I can't believe that they're trying to teach us handwriting! "), picking up those fragrant gym bags, singing and playing and directing band music, and eating at every possible juncture of life. The cupcakes with Frost-ing and the eyeball cookies remain as cherished gustatory landmarks.

The next year was spent in snatches of conversation during the changing of classes and reports from Mr. Houghton on your many virtues. Using his hand to shield his mouth to prevent passersby from hearing this privileged information, Mr. Houghton would talk about your most recent projects or question some idiosyncrasy that had astonished him. He often mentioned examples of fine writing, laughing about Nathan and his forgetfulness of possessions. The year seemed to have a paler color to it, or perhaps I was just hungry more often. I missed the no-holds-barred quality of life that we had created in our unique society, and you, who could tell if you missed anything? You were still leaders, speaking broadly and gesturing grandly, and your voices flung down the hall were never indistinct.

Came the tenth grade, and <u>Eternity in Their Hearts</u>. You were stunned and indignant at such writing and so unreasonable an assignment. Christine joined me in mocking the exclamation points, and somewhere along the line the Michelles put the books down. You found out that, along with having to read, "the hardest, dumbest book in the world" according to Jennifer, your literature book was the heaviest, and mutiny was in the air. Just about the time that Chad and Company were hauling in the gangplank and Becky was unfolding the blindfold, IT happened. Applying the truth of that book to your hearts, the Holy Spirit gave you both a break and a wake-up call. I can recall your faces when you had that "Eureka!" experience for which I had planned and prayed, and God was real to you in a stunning way. God did what He said He would do, and you chewed on that for days. The skits were born of that newly-found maturity, and from that book was born your framework of understanding the other literature. Over and over I'd look up to see the connection remade as you read some line from an assignment and His faithfulness was reborn for you again. Carrie's slow smile and "Yeah, I get it" accompanied your nodding heads (some in agreement, some in attempted slumber), and once again we saw that God did what He said He would, this time in your lives.

Ordered Steps

Fall, 1994, my long-awaited cherubs and the world's most exciting curriculum arrived, and with it new citizens of assorted sizes, shapes, and sounds. The year was inaugurated by impassioned, oft interrupted discussions of art and truth and beauty and spirituality, and that was just the first day. Jack rolled his eyes at me from his unexpectedly lofty vantage point, and Janell took more notes than did the rest of the entire class.

The world views concept beat us all up for a while, and then that clicking thing happened, and romanticism was inhaled in one moment. Laura's desk developed a magnetic attraction to another's, and I found myself acting as the social Berlin Wall.

Presentations were pursued unintentionally, if at all, and then, boom! Senior alumnae of the world views class remarked with knowing smiles about overheard conversations as you passed, and Becky would wave her arms about and moan, "So many books, so little time!" It was terrifying and exhilarating and inspirational. Carrie apologized to the Unitarians for her lack of interest in their church, and Christine visited a real live commune. Voracious in your appetites, you sifted through jewelry, movies, music, clothes, cartoons, and speeches for the rest of the year, snatching up identifiable elements and dragging their lifeless bodies to class for group dissection. Even Bryan, who is famous for staying out of our insanity, designed an Underoos world view in our frenzy of knowledge. And then, without warning, our year was over. Your heads bent over the exam and my eyes strained over yearbooks. We spent our last days too busy, or perhaps just too unwilling, to lament. So, Mrs.

Wilkerson, you were right. The process is the point. The new Luther print in the office doesn't mention our happy band by name, but it is us, consumed with the business of becoming.

We are, as the song says, His sanctuary, and while the construction may be painful, it is on-going. May the passersby always recognize our Architect.

Personal-type note:

It has been my pleasure to torture, uh, teach you this year. Watching you grow in your faith, intellect -- and heart (not to mention writing) -- has been a regular source of joy. I love you.

Mrs. Zappulla

Previously Published

The following essays are reprinted from indicated sources.

"Four Yellow Chairs," Christian Educators Journal, Nd, p. 5.

"Lessons from Chas," Christian Educators Journal, Oct-Nov. 1989, 30-31.

"No Longer John Wayne. "Christian Educators Journal, Feb-Mar, 1990, 24-25.

"To Be the Parent of An Abused Child, "School Counselor, May 1993, 40(35-   36).

"When I Grow Up, I Want To Be Just Like. Who?" http:/www. Corrections.com.(5/1/2010).

"When Reading Became Cool ... Accidentally," http:/www.Corrections.com. (5/10/2010).

Made in the USA
Columbia, SC
22 April 2020